G000055353

MAKING FOR THE OPEN

By the same author

A Strange Girl in Bright Colours
Unplayed Music
Star Whisper

Direct Dialling (Chatto & Windus)

MAKING FOR THE OPEN
The Chatto Book of Post-Feminist Poetry 1964–1984

Carol Rumens

CHATTO & WINDUS · THE HOGARTH PRESS

LONDON

Published in 1985 by
Chatto & Windus · The Hogarth Press
40 William IV Street
London WC2N 4DF

All rights reserved. No part of this publication may be reproduced, stored in a retrieval system, or transmitted, in any form, or by any means, electronic, mechanical, photocopying, recording or otherwise, without the prior permission of the publisher.

British Library Cataloguing in Publication Data
Making for the open: the Chatto book of post-feminist poetry 1964–1984.
    1. Poetry – Women authors 2. Poetry, Modern – 20th century
I. Rumens, Carol
808.81   PN6109.9

ISBN 0–7011–2848–8

Selection and Introduction copyright © Carol Rumens 1985

Phototypeset by Wyvern Typesetting Limited, Bristol
Printed in Great Britain by
Redwood Burn Ltd., Trowbridge, Wiltshire

For David Rumens

CONTENTS

Introduction page xv

U. A. FANTHORPE
The Passing of Alfred 3
Father in the Railway Buffet 4
The Constant Tin Soldier 4

ANNE STEVENSON
By the Boat House, Oxford 12
Thales and Li Po 12
A Summer Place 13
Suicide 14

ELIZABETH BARTLETT
W. E. A. Course 15
Loving Neighbour 16

FLEUR ADCOCK
Blue Glass 17
Dreaming 19
Madmen 19

VICKI FEAVER
Mr Sparke 20
Teddy-bears 22

PATRICIA BEER
The Customer at the Ship Inn 22
Jury Duty 23
Overseas Student 24
Lemmings 25

JEAN EARLE
The Roof 26
Times of Turn Round 27
Nanternis 27

WENDY COPE
A Policeman's Lot 28
Strugnell's Sonnets 1 & 2 29

ELMA MITCHELL
Late Fall 30
Thoughts After Ruskin 31
Instead of a Flag 32

SELIMA HILL
Below Hekla 33
The Fowlers of the Marshes 34

ALISON BRACKENBURY
Medine in Turkey 34
Two Gardeners 35

GWEN HARWOOD
David's Harp 36
The Sea Anemones 38

ANTIGONE KEFALA
The Place 38

JILL HELLYER
Living With Aunts 40

DOROTHY HEWETT
Legend of the Green Country 41

ANNA SWIRSZCZYNSKA
She Can't Sleep 50
He Treats them to Ice-cream 51
Peasant Woman 51
Family Life 52
Two Old Women 52
The Reaper 52
Her Greatest Love 52

ASTRIDE IVASKA
To the Memory of a Poet 53
That Which has Remained Unlived 54

ANA BLANDIANA
Links 54

GABRIELA MELINESCU
Birth 55

NATALYA GORBANEVSKAYA
'Wipe the bliss . . .' 55
Three Poems on the Road 56
'And you . . .' 57
'Something's with me . . .' 57

BELLA AKHMADULINA
Fever 58
Small Aircraft 62

YUNNA MORITZ
Midday in Gantiadi 63
'Now we'll go' 63

NOVELLA MATVEYEVA
The Eggplants have Pins and Needles 64

MARIANNE MOORE
The Mind, Intractable Thing 65
Dream 66
Enough 67

ELIZABETH BISHOP
The Moose 67
One Art 72

ADRIENNE RICH
Dialogue 73
For a Russian Poet 74
Jerusalem 76

MARILYN HACKER
La Vie de Château 77
Villanelle 78
The Last Time 79

BARBARA GUEST
Circassians 80
Roses 82
Even Ovid 83
The Interruptions 84

LOUISE GLÜCK
Gratitude 85
Flowering Plum 86

CELIA GILBERT
Clyde 86
The Silence 87

BEATRICE HAWLEY
Stones 88
The Wife's Poem 89

AMY CLAMPITT
Stacking the Straw 90
Tepoztlán 91
Salvage 93

CAROLYN FORCHÉ
The Memory of Elena 94
The Visitor 95
Departure 95
The Colonel 96

CLARIBEL ALEGRÍA
Everything is Normal in our Backyard 97
The American Way of Death 99

KATHLEEN JAMIE
Black Spiders 101
Storm in Istanbul 101

VALERIE GILLIES
Bomber 102
Harrowing 103

LIZ LOCHHEAD
Poppies 104
My Rival's House 105

ÁGNES GERGELY
Crazed Man in Concentration Camp 106
Sign on My Door Jamb 107

MARGARET ATWOOD
The Reincarnation of Captain Cook 108
The Shadow Voice 109
The Surveyors 110
At The Tourist Centre in Boston 111

MIRIAM WADDINGTON
What is a Canadian 112
Beau-Belle 112
Back at York University 113
Popular Geography 114

JENNY MASTORÁKI
The Vandals 115
Prometheus 115
The Death of a Warrior 116

DAHLIA RAVIKOVITCH
The Horns of Hittin 116
Deep Calleth unto Deep 118

RIVKA MIRIAM
The Stripes in Joseph's Coat 118
Miriam's Well 119
Die in Me 119
The Girl Who Drowned in the Well 120

EUNICE DE SOUZA
Marriages Are Made 120
He Speaks 121
Autobiographical 122

SARAH KIRSCH
Before the Sun Rises 123
Dogtooth Violet Marsh Trefoil 123
Noon 124

HELGA M. NOVAK
Punishment – Another Look 124
What a Wind 125

BETTINA WEGNER
The Enemy 126

ÉILEAN NÍ CHUILLEANÁIN
Acts and Monuments 127
Wash 127
More Islands 128

MEDBH MCGUCKIAN
Confinement 129
To the Nightingale 129
Vanessa's Bower 130
From the Dressing-room 130

EAVAN BOLAND
Naoise at Four 131
On Renoir's 'The Grape Pickers' 132
After a Childhood away from Ireland 133

VLADIMÍRA ČEREPKOVÁ
Man and his Truth 134

GERDA MAYER
Monkey on the Analyst's Couch 135
15th March 1939 135
Poem About Something 136

DESANKA MAKSIMOVIĆ
For Lies Spoken out of Kindness 137
Now it is Certain 137

VESNA PARUN
A House on the Road 138

GRACE NICHOLS
Wind a Change 139
The Return 139
Like Anansi 140
Old Magic 140
Waterpot 141

RUTH MILLER
Fruit 142
Penguin on the Beach 142

Contributors' notes 145

Acknowledgements 149

INTRODUCTION

Since the feminist renaissance of the nineteen-sixties, many anthologies of women poets have been published in Britain and the USA. Few have been solely, or even primarily, concerned with excellence, and, like many other readers, I have reacted with mixed feelings: pleasure at seeing so many women in print, delight at the occasional discovery or rediscovery of talent, but, more often than not, disappointment with the quality of the work. The political orientation of much women's publishing (without which, of course, it would not have come into being) has sometimes, particularly in the case of poetry, led to the elevation of the message at the expense of the medium. Those writers concerned with 'the stern art of poetry' as an end in itself have tended to be swamped by the noisy amateurs proclaiming that women, too, have a voice. This anthology is different from its predecessors in that the poems proclaim only themselves. That women have a voice, and the right to be heard, goes without saying.

In this sense, then, the volume is 'post-feminist'. The term is certainly not meant to suggest that Utopia has arrived, and that all is now milk and honey for the once-oppressed. Neither should it be thought that the starting date of the anthology implies the view that there were no further developments in feminist thinking or social reform after 1964. Such a view would clearly be absurd. However, it would be equally absurd to claim that no significant changes, radically affecting many women (particularly those of the middle, i.e. writing classes) had not occurred by 1964. The rise of the general level of education, the advent of birth-control by contraception or, in Eastern Europe, abortion, the fashionable, but important, questioning of social stereotypes initiated in the late nineteen-fifties when the 'youth culture' first began to blossom, are among the contributing factors. As for the philosophy of feminism, it should only be necessary to mention a few names – Mary Wollstonecraft, John Stuart Mill, Rebecca West, Virginia Woolf, Simone de Beauvoir spring instantly to mind, and there are many more – to remind the feminists of the nineteen-seventies and eighties that their movement has a long and distinguished history.

During the period covered by *Making for the Open*, more women poets of quality have emerged than at any other time. The reason is clear. Language can be used authentically (and poetry is language at its most authentic) only by those whose existence, whose *being*, is authentic. 'Post-feminist' expresses a psychological, rather than political, condition, though its roots are no doubt political. It implies a mental freedom which a few outstanding women in any age have achieved, and which many more, with increasing confidence, are claiming today.

Few women writers can be indifferent to the issues of feminism. Their dilemma can perhaps be illuminated by looking at the far more serious dilemma of those writers attempting to work within a totalitarian dictatorship (some of whom are included in this book). In such a society, the writer can be as crippled by the demand to work against the establishment as to work within it. An interesting essay by the Peruvian novelist, Mario Vargas Llosa, entitled 'The Writer in Latin America' in *They Shoot Writers, Don't They?*, ed. George Theiner (Faber, 1984), examines the problem in some detail. 'The congenital unsubmissiveness of literature', says Llosa, 'is much broader than is believed by those who consider it a mere instrument for opposing governments and dominating social structures; it strikes equally at everything which stands for dogma and logical exclusivism in the interpretation of life, that is, both ideological orthodoxies and heterodoxies. In other words, it is a living, systematic, inevitable contradiction of all that exists.'

This is not of course to say that no man or woman can be 'cradled into poetry by wrong'. A number of the poems in this anthology clearly derive emotional force from an intense political or social engagement: those of Natalya Gorbanevskaya, Carolyn Forché, Claribel Alegría, Adrienne Rich, and Grace Nichols, for example. Their manner ranges from the directly outspoken to the highly oblique. Nevertheless, it is clear that for even the most committed of these writers, the art of the poem is of vital importance. Technique has not been abandoned because of the seriousness of the message.

Making for the Open contains work from twenty countries, with, for obvious reasons, a preponderance of British and American writers. While limiting my chronological field to the last two decades, I have been concerned both to represent women poets of an earlier generation who have continued to produce interesting work within this period (Marianne Moore and Desanka Maksimović, for example) and those who have more recently emerged. If confronted, for reasons of space, with the choice between an established and a new poet of equal interest, however, I have usually opted for the latter. Because the number of eligible poets turned out to be dauntingly, if enthrallingly, large, omissions have been inevitable. I have left out several poets already well-represented in anthologies – Stevie Smith, Elizabeth Jennings, Kathleen Raine, Frances Horovitz, for instance; some who would not wish to be identified as 'post-feminist'; and others who seem to me at their best when read in substantial amounts. (As every anthologist knows, not all poets and not all poems are at their most effective in a mixed bouquet.) Then there are the younger poets of obvious talent who have still to produce their best work.

My aim was not merely to display the technical accomplishment of women writers but to indicate something of the sheer range and variety of subject matter. In that much-anthologised poem 'A Bookshop Idyll', Kingsley Amis paid women a backhanded compliment in suggesting that their poems were more likely than men's to express emotion, less likely to proclaim 'I think', 'I travel', 'I read'. The poems in this volume are proof to anyone who still needs it that such activities are not entirely unknown among women. On the other hand, there can be no poetry without feelings; the objective, 'masculine' poem is, of course, a mythical beast. Again, as far as subject matter is concerned, I have made no attempt to discriminate against poems dealing with specifically female experiences, provided they are genuine poems – as, for example, 'Thoughts After Ruskin' by Elma Mitchell and the 'I am Baba' poems by Anna Swirszczynska certainly are.

This brings me to the matter of poems in translation. I am well aware of the extraordinary difficulties of this complex art; I still think it is one well worth undertaking, and perhaps even essential to human survival. Naturally I have limited my selection to those poems which seem to me to be effective as 'English' poems. Unfortunately, because it usually takes a considerable time for a poet's work to filter into other languages and cultures, my selection can be no more than a tiny sample of what has been written comparatively recently in a limited number of languages. Availability has been one deciding factor, translatability another. For example, reading among the relatively small number of French women poets in English, I was not finally convinced that any of the translations was wholly successful as an 'English' poem. Conversely, Russian poetry has always seemed peculiarly amenable to English translations – or perhaps it is simply that it has tended to attract the best translators. This balance is reflected in the anthology. Four Russian poets are included, and a smaller sample of work from Israel, El Salvador, Greece, Poland, Latvia, Romania, Hungary, East Germany, Yugoslavia and Czechoslovakia.

Like the feminist anthologies before it, *Making for the Open* began with an act of positive discrimination. This seems to me morally justifiable on the grounds that those who have suffered negative discrimination deserve some righting of the balance, and artistically defensible on the grounds that an anthology, if it is to be readable, must have some limiting factor, that of gender being as good a one as any. I hope the fact that the women represented here are, first and foremost, good poets will be noted equally by those who think there are no women poets of any merit, and by those generous souls who believe that women should be judged by less than stringent measurements of excellence. Above all, I hope the book might prove to be a small stepping-stone to the time when we do not feel obliged to think of writers in terms of gender at all. Post-feminism, then, will be more than merely a state of mind.

MAKING FOR THE OPEN

U. A. FANTHORPE

The Passing of Alfred

'He [Tennyson] died with his hand on his Shakespeare, and the moon
shining full into the window over him . . . A worthy end.'
  Queen Victoria: *Journal*

Our fathers were good at dying.
They did it lingeringly,
As if they liked it; correctly,
With earnest attention to detail,
Codicils brought up to date,
Forgiveness, confession, last-gasp
Penitence properly witnessed
By responsible persons. Attorneys,
Clerics, physicians, all knew their place
In the civil pavane of dying.

Households discharged
Their methodical duties: said farewell
In order of precedence, outdoor staff first,
Faithful hounds respectfully mourning,
Lastly the widow-to-be, already
Pondering a transformed wardrobe.

They died in the houses,
The beds they were born in,
They died where they lived, between
Known sheets, to the obbligato
Of familiar creaks and ticks.

We who differ, whose dears are absorbed
Into breezy wards for routine terminations,
Envy our fathers their decorous endings
In error. Nothing makes extinction easy.
They also died appallingly, over
The family breakfast-cups; bloodily
In childbed; graveyard coughed themselves
Into coffins; declined from heart-break
And hunger. And however resigned,

Orderly, chaste, aesthetic the passing of Alfred,
Remorse, regret still shadowed the living after.

Like us they ran from habit to tell good news
To dead ears; like us they dreamed
Of childhood, and being forgiven;
And the dead followed them, as they do us,
Tenderly through darkness,
But fade when we turn to look in the upper air.

Father in the Railway Buffet

What are you doing here, ghost, among these urns,
These film-wrapped sandwiches and help-yourself biscuits,
Upright and grand, with your stick, hat and gloves,
Your breath of eau-de-cologne?

What have you to say to these head-scarfed tea-ladies,
For whom your expensive vowels are exotic as Japan?
Stay, ghost, in your proper haunts, the clubland smokerooms,
Where you know the waiters by name.

You have no place among these damp and nameless.
Why do you walk here? *I came to say goodbye.*
You were ashamed of me for being different.
It didn't matter.

You who never even learned to queue?

The Constant Tin Soldier

1. BREAKING DAY

Dying is easier.
Just a flick of somebody's finger,
Then the icy exactness of rigor mortis,
While posthumous flies and decorations settle,
A subaltern writes thirty-two letters
By torchlight to next of kin,
And the Germans advance in your boots,
Which are better than theirs.

It isn't always lucky to stay alive.
Some never recover from surviving.
The showy heraldry of scars excuses,
But not the chronic tic of terror,
Picked up on a foggy March morning
Between the Staffords and the Suffolks,
Between Bullecourt and Croisilles.
You will carry this day like a tumour
In your head for life, fusilier,
And no one will ever needle it out.

You remember the date:

21st March, 1918. Day
Of the Kaiserschlacht, day
Of the German Spring Offensive.
We, the beaten, have no name for that day
In our own language.

You remember your place:

Third Army, 34th Division,
102nd brigade. HQ Gomiecourt
(Which I never saw) under
Lt Col Charlton (whom I never
Saw again after. Only now, sixty years on,
A youngster tells me he was taken prisoner.
I thought him killed).
23rd Northumberland Fusiliers.

You remember the weather:

Sun on the 20th, following rain
And squally winds. Enemy weathermen
Prophesied continuing calm. It would be safe,
They said, to use gas against us. Then
An intense, still morning; no wind;
But ground mist ghosting
To dense, inimical fog.

You remember the timing:

0440 hours: artillery bombardment begins.
Five hours of General Surprise Fire.
The German brass, guns, mortars and howitzers,
Jarring in unison. It rained noise,
Mud, bone, hot lumps of jagged metal,
Gas, smoke, fear, darkness, dissolution
By the clock, if any clock ticked on.
0940 hours: infantry attack begins,
Across the broken earth, the broken men.
An orderly advance; they sauntered
Over the unstrung landscape.

You remember your state:

Fear, fog, solitude,
Between Bullecourt and Croisilles,
Between the Staffords and the Suffolks.
We had to man the Forward Zone,
But creeping with the creeping fog
Came in the enemy. We knew them
By the shape of their helmets. They were
Where we were. Nothing was where
It had been on the map, and no one
Was one of us. The counties melted,
And their quiet local voices. My friend
Died, I was on my own.

You remember your mood:

Orphaned. The formal beauty
Of rank, its cordial courteous bearing,
Had foundered. No one to give
Or receive orders. Our training
Was scrappy; we had never studied
The delicate art of retreat, and our trumpets
Had mud in their throats.

You remember your choice:

Flight. Through craters, corpses,
Stumps of horses, guns and trees,
Through fog and my everyman darkness.
What are the rules for the solitary
Soldier? Should he stand firm
To the last pointless volley,
Or lay down his arms at the feet
Of kind enemies, and be whisked
By their finished techniques
To a snug internment? No one
Had drilled enterprise into us.
Choice had been frightened to death.
I could do only what I did,
What the primitive man I muzzle
Inside me made me do: I ran.

You remember the sequel:

Rehabilitation. The comfort of being
Among confederates, men
Who had hobbled their way back, stubbornly,
Without heroism. Most of us still
Had our uses. Mine was liaison
With American troops. Gigantic,
Buoyant, ignorant, they trod
Our shellshocked fief, as once their ancestors
Trampled across the New World.
I guided them along the labyrinths,
Interpreted, explained, a ghost of war,
Leading the living down the dead men's trenches.

You remember your self:

I had archaic longings,
Yearned for the dead and the lost,
The officers, the other ranks, the men
I belonged with, who knew the same songs,
Shouted on United. Not even
Graves for most, just Memorials
To the Missing. I missed them,

All the canny Geordie lads
With their feet still through the night
And the days.

2. SPOILS OF PEACE
Some of the dead were signallers:
Rupert the Fair and Wilfred the Wise,
Isaac the exile and innocent Ivor,
And Edward, who endured.

In various ways, these died,
And so, afterwards, in some ways,
Some of the living perhaps listened.

The dead can afford to be generous,
Having no superannuation rights.
These men squandered the spoils of war,
But I latched on to my red-edged learning,

Investing sensibly in job, house, car,
Wife and children, dog and skivvy.
Redoubts and outworks, manned by me,
To balk the enemy at my back.

I couldn't afford to be taken
The same way twice; kept short accounts,
Checked the wiring, planted sharp roses,
Trained the dog to the qui vive.

But upkeep has to be paid for. I traded
My craftsman's hands for a salesman's pay.
Built my house on my tongue. Charm
Was the mortar, the brickwork cheek.

In a world fit for heroes, heroism
Is de trop. You have to fight
With guile for your rights, against
The agenda-adept, the minutes-men.

I mastered the means that made men mine,
Not shadows, to fade in the gassed thicket,

But beefy reliable cheque-signing fingers,
Dewlaps to dance at my bagman's patter.

I held the line, from Wallsend to Workington,
Where the Romans were, I came.
Chatted up waitresses, chaffed the barmen,
Sold my soul to keep myself safe.

(Not between Croisilles and Bullecourt.)

Good morning!
                Good gracious!
                                Nice day.
                                        Delightful.
Any tonics, tinctures or pick-me-ups?
No.
Thank you. I'll call again.
                Good morning.
                                Nice day.

Where the wind whips over the fraying border,
Where homesick legions were whittled away,
On the frontier of failure I jobbed and prospered,
Natty, dapper, with my quickfire smile.
Not the dovetailed sockets, the tonguing and grooving,
The crisscross network I could have carved,
But a web of hardheaded sceptical buyers,
Whom I forced at jokepoint to be my friends.

Good morning!
                Good morning.
                                Nice day.
                                        Yes.
Any false rumours, horrors or hangovers?
No thank you.
I'll call again.
        Do.
                Good morning.
                                Good morning.

Shocking day.

Back at HQ the walls stood firm.
I saw to that. But the garrison
Could never be trusted. Maids
Came and went, children were born

And died. The dog too. I procured
Replacements, held weekly inspections,
Reviewed morale, kept up my payments,
Insured house, contents and livestock, checked

The defences. There was nothing amiss.
But somehow I had enlisted
A saboteur, not a friend (my friend
Died). She gave me nothing

To complain of; collaborated in all
Transactions, performed creditably
At trade functions, answered the telephone
Adequately. But I didn't like

The sort of book she read. Disaffection
Was plain in her children. The boy

A myopic coward, whose only solution
Was running away. Then the girl

Who died. I forget her name now,
But she cost me a mint of money
At the time, one way and the other.
As for the substitute, I recognised

A usurper in her. She'd have ousted
Me, taken my place if she could,
Mutinous, sulky, and damnably
Heir to my look and my hands.

I had carved out a kingdom
For my son to inherit. But he
Renegued, would have none of it,
Fancied his own improvident way,

Instead of cultivating my contacts.
Married a fatherless, unsuitable
Outspoken girl from down south somewhere,
Ran to the opposite end of the earth

And stayed there. Good riddance.
One less mouth to feed, one less craven
In the camp. The girl deserted too,
After a prolonged, costly education

Without a dividend. No hope there
Of a son-in-law, someone I could
Have trusted, canny chap, living close,
To keep an eye on the wiring, the blood-pressure,

Someone I could have taken to, without
That yellow streak in him. But I managed
Without. Anticipated the next assault
(Infirmity, loneliness, death) and took

Precautionary measures: transferred HQ
To a high-rise residence for the well-heeled,
Heated centrally, caretakered, with lift,
Where care would be taken.

Here we live now, annuitied. I ignore
The persistent trickle of offstage
Deaths, as my feebler contemporaries
Fall out. Life has taught me
To concentrate on living. This I do.

My primitive man is dead, crushed
By cordial years of cronies. I couldn't
Speak straight now if I tried.
I am the kerbside cheapjack's patter:

Ladies, watch what I do.
The genuine article. 20 pound in the catalogue,
18 in the shops, 15 in the sales. But from me –
Stand close, ladies – *a fiver*!
Ladies, watch what I do.

Watch, ladies, what I do.
Holidays abroad yearly, until age
Made us uninsurable. Now a five-star
Scottish hydro, where I am known

To the management. I am still standing to,
Between the Staffords and the Suffolks,
As I have been for most of my life.
I may be only a tin soldier,
But I have been constant.

ANNE STEVENSON

By the Boat House, Oxford

They belong here in their own quenched country.
I had forgotten nice women could be so nice,
smiling beside large sons on the makeshift quay,
frail, behind pale faces and hurt eyes.

Their husbands are plainly superior, with them, without them.
Their boys wear privilege like a clear inheritance, easily.
(Now a swan's neck couples with its own reflection,
making in the simple water a perfect 3.)

The punts seem resigned to an unexciting mooring.
But the women? It's hard to tell. Do their fine grey hairs
and filament lips approve or disdain the loving
that living alone, or else lonely in pairs, impairs?

Thales and Li Po

Thales, out
scanning the stars for truth,
walked into a well.
Li Po fell in love
with the moon's
reflection
in the Yellow River.

Which was the right way to die?
It doesn't matter.
Try an analysis of sky
or, passionate, ignorant,
embrace a lie.

A Summer Place

You know that house she called home,
so sleek, so clapboard-white,
that used to be some country jobber's blight
or scab on our hill's arm.
You can see the two cellars of the barn,
stones still squatting where the fellow stacked them.

He worked the place as a farm,
though how, with stones for soil, she never knew.
Partly she hoped he'd been a poet, too —
why else hang Haystack mountain and its view
from north-west windows?
It was the view she bought it for. He'd gone.
The house sagged on its frame. The barns were down.

The use she saw for it was not to be
of use. A summer place. A lovely
setting where fine minds could graze
at leisure on long summer days
and gather books from bushes, phrase by phrase.
Work would be thought. A tractor bought for play
would scare unnecessary ugly scrub away.

A white gem set on a green silk glove
she bought and owned there.
And summers wore it, just as she would wear
each summer like a dress of sacred air
until the house was half compounded of
foundations, beams and paint, half of her love.

She lived profoundly, felt, wrote from her heart,
knew each confessional songbird by its voice,

cloistered her garden with bee balm and fanning iris,
sat, stained by sunsets in a vault of noise
listening through cricket prayer for whitethroat,
hermit thrush – and couldn't keep it out,
the shade of something wrong, a fear, a doubt,

as though she heard the house stir in its plaster,
stones depart unsteadily from walls,
the woods, unwatched, stretch out their roots like claws
and tear through careful fences, fiercer than saws.
Something alive lived under her mind-cropped pasture,
hated the house – or worse, loved, hungering after
its perfectly closed compactness, breathed disaster.

She dreamed or daydreamed what it might have come to,
the house itself, wanting the view
to take it, and the view's love gathering into
brambles, tendrils, trunks of maples, needing
her every window, entering, seeding . . .
Fear of attack kept her from sleeping,
kept her awake in her white room, pacing, weeping.

But you see the place still stands there, pretty as new.
Whatever she thought the mountain and trees would do,
they did – and took her with them – and withdrew.

Suicide

There was no hole in the universe to fit him.
He felt it as he fooled around. No rim,
no closet, nowhere to hide. The moon
also was fooling. He told
the girl and she giggled. 'As much for you
as for anyone.' But it wasn't true.

Spiders with their eight eyes, snails had more to do.

'When I said I wouldn't kiss him
he said he'd slash his wrists.
He was always saying stupid things like this.'

He saw himself entering women.
Wide open hay-scented barn, transistor on,
heavy rhythm of drums to draw him in.
And then that smallness, tiny loop at the end
where a slipknot tightened over light until a fist
struck. Darkness swelled around him like a breast.

The noose around his neck had been some help –
a childish mouth, a joke, an easy jump.
He was free as air when the girl's father found him,
returning from an evening out with friends.

ELIZABETH BARTLETT

W. E. A. Course

This evening we are doing Pasternak.
Last week we did Alexander Solzhenitsyn.
Outside this room which has wall to wall carpets
And stands illuminated in its own grounds,
The English autumn dies, modest and well-mannered,
The leaves swept away from the drive, the sun still warm
During the daylight hours, warmth reflected upon the face
Of our tutor, who could be my son, and looks like
D. H. Lawrence.
They should have warned me of Simochka
Who sits on my right in fashionable clothes,
And long blond hair, or Nerzhin,
Who was transferred at the end of chapter nine.
We sit in a circle, but Dante would not have recognized us
As persons with grave and tranquil eyes and great
Authority in our carriage and attitude.
This proves we have actually read The First Circle,
But this week I am glad to have travelled
The long train journey without Omar Sharif,
And seen the candles burn, and the iced rowanberries.
Across the room sits Lara, rather silent and also
A librarian, and next to her the Public Prosecutor.

Outside the wind is blowing, and the snow blocks out
This commuter town, silting against the door.
We are trapped, we cannot escape, we grovel
For a few potatoes, a few logs of wood.
Red specks and threads of blood gleam on the snow,
And the sound of gun-fire ends the class as we flee
In cars and on bicycles with our books under our arms.
Next week to Sicily with Lampedusa,
Nunc et in hora mortis nostrae. Amen,
And I shall be cast for the Leopard's wife,
Gesummaria, how far away the snow will seem.
It will be hot wherever we are, and Bendico
Will follow me home through the neon-lighted streets,
His dust will crumble and his smell pursue me,
As Komarovsky pursues me now, in his green car,
Dark as the forests at Varykino, cold as a Russian
Winter, in this Michaelmas weather, cruel and ruthless
As the unseasonable revolution we are all waiting for,
With only a grammar of feeling to defend us.
Ah, Yury, the snow is falling, the stars have gone,
And I am alone; we are lost to each other forever.

Loving Neighbour

This summer, the unfamiliar sea, and the driftwood
Leaning against the wall in the sun, and the pile
Of kindling grown too big, because the letter says work,
Because the letter says stoop and carry,
Drag the wood from the cargo ships a mile
Over the rocks, and you may miscarry.

The sea has deprived the happy pregnant women
Of their golden oranges. They rot in the sand
Among the broken crates and the twisted branches,
And the bloated life-belts under this sultry
Summer sky, but the letter says work, do not stand
And think, but work, and cancel out adultery.

These long weeks the sea has been too calm,
The sun too bright and regular to hold my pain.
Even the letter says storm and the waves beating,
For the letter says work, and the storm brings wood,
And flings it along the shore, bright paint and salt stain,
Pattern and chaos, and sodden food.

To-night, the bell-buoy out in the bay,
And the gulls' feet pattering on the tiles:
And the path to the sands trodden hard,
And the house swept clean, because I may not marry.
But the letter says get up, add to the pile
Of kindling, and you may miscarry.

I do not know why the gulls are silent,
There is no colour in the sea and the sands are empty and clean.
In my belly your storm advances,
But my mind is as calm as this strange sad summer has been.

Where is my loving neighbour? Who will help me to bed?
The sea is my loving neighbour, and the sand shifts under my
    head.
No-one gathers driftwood by moonlight,
But I have done what the letter said.

FLEUR ADCOCK

Blue Glass

The underworld of children becomes the overworld
when Janey or Sharon shuts the attic door
on a sunny afternoon and tiptoes in sandals
that softly waffle-print the dusty floor

to the cluttered bed below the skylight,
managing not to sneeze as she lifts
newspapers, boxes, gap-stringed tennis-racquets
and a hamster's cage to the floor, and shifts

the tasselled cover to make a clean surface
and a pillow to be tidy under her head
before she straightens, mouths the dark sentence,
and lays herself out like a mummy on the bed.

Her wrists are crossed. The pads of her fingertips
trace the cold glass emblem where it lies
like a chain of hailstones melting in the dips
above her collarbones. She needs no eyes

to see it: the blue bead necklace, of sapphire
or lapis, or of other words she knows
which might mean blueness: amethyst, azure,
chalcedony can hardly say how it glows.

She stole it. She tells herself that she found it.
It's hers now. It owns her. She slithers among
its globular teeth, skidding on blue pellets.
Ice-beads flare and blossom on her tongue,

turn into flowers, populate the spaces
around and below her. The attic has become
her bluebell wood. Among their sappy grasses
the light-fringed gas-flames of bluebells hum.

They lift her body like a cloud of petals.
High now, floating, this is what she sees:
granular bark six inches from her eyeballs;
the wood of rafters is the wood of trees.

Her breathing moistens the branches' undersides;
the sunlight in an interrupted shaft
warms her legs and lulls her as she rides
on air, a slender and impossible raft

of bones and flesh; and whether it is knowledge
or a limpid innocence on which she feeds
for power hasn't mattered. She turns the necklace
kindly in her fingers, and soothes the beads.

Dreaming

'Oblivion, that's all. I never dream,' he said –
proud of it, another immunity,
another removal from the standard frame which she
inhabited, dreaming beside him of a dead
woman tucked neatly into a small bed,
a cot or a child's bunk, unexpectedly
victim of some friend or lover. 'Comfort me,'
said the dreamer, 'I need to be comforted.'
He did that, not bothering to comprehend,
and she returned to her story: a doctor came
to identify the placid corpse in her dream.
It was obscure; but glancing towards the end
she guessed that killer and lover and doctor were the same;
proving that things are ultimately what they seem.

Madmen

Odd how the seemingly maddest of men –
sheer loonies, the classically paranoid,
violently possessive about their secrets,
whispered after from corners, terrified
of poison in their coffee, driven frantic
(whether for or against him) by discussion of God,
peculiar, to say the least, about their mothers –
return to their gentle senses in bed.

Suddenly straightforward, they perform
with routine confidence, neither afraid
that their partner will turn and bite their balls off
nor groping under the pillow for a razor-blade;
eccentric only in their conversation,
which rambles on about the meaning of a word
they used in an argument in 1969,
they leave their women grateful, relieved, and bored.

VICKI FEAVER

Mr Sparke

In memoriam Annie Sparke

I

It was the worst winter in memory
his neighbour tells us, smoothing out
a cutting from the *Hexham Courant* –
a picture of already yellowing whiteness –
as if she thinks we don't believe her.

But we can see for ourselves: the grass
has hardly grown; spring flowers are late
coming through and in a dip behind the far wood
there's a swathe of hard grey snow
with pine needles frozen in like splinters.

Up at Allenheads, she says, a man
who'd lived there all his life
and must have known the dangers
left his car and was buried in a drift.
They thought he'd have to have his hand off.

She'd been worried Mrs Sparke
would wander out again and be lost.
That's why she called the doctor.
Her husband dug a tunnel to the phone box –
It was like standing in an igloo.

The snow was piled so high
they had to stand on chairs to watch
for the ambulance from the window.
And after that they were cut off for weeks.
He never saw her again.

2

Mr Sparke's garden is as trim as ever.
The narrow borders by the path
are lined with scarlet tulips;

the soil is freshly dug and raked
ready for potatoes and the first seeds.

Dressed in his dark blue Sunday suit
he calls to us – not as we'd expected
to sit with him in gloomy sympathy
but to admire (what must have cost him most
of the insurance) a new cassette recorder.

At the centre of the old oak sideboard,
flanked by two china shepherdesses,
it seems oddly out of place.
Like a child showing off a new toy
he won't let us go until we've heard it.

While he twists the silver buttons
we wait, uncomfortably, exchanging looks,
remembering those bulging watery eyes,
her matted unwashed hair,
the conversations leading nowhere.

He'd never seemed to notice she was ill.
He just kept on at that wall –
covering the stones with cement;
drawing the shapes of stones
on the smooth surface.

We try to think of an excuse to go.
But suddenly like ice melting in a thaw
the sound begins to flow –
an accordion band squeezing out
'What a friend we have in Jesus'.

And Mr Sparke is crying; rubbing
at his eyes with a work-swollen hand.
'What I always say is,' he shouts
above the noise: 'It's my belief
that time's a great healer.'

Teddy-bears

After years in the cold
the teddy-bears have come back to bed;
brought out of the cupboard under the stairs
like gods completely forgotten
when the times were good.

They're an amiable pair –
a couple of comedians in a silent film,
the sort of companions who don't complain
at losing an eye or an ear,
at having the stuffing knocked out of them.

They are philosophic
about the way life treats them:
even, it seems, about the intruder
who just as they must have begun to think
they were permanent fixtures

dislodges them from the pillow
to involve them in a game in which
with noses pressed into the eiderdown
they are 'teddy-bears star-gazing',
or propped dizzily on their heads

'teddy-bears trying to remember something'.
They are souls of discretion.
In the morning we find them
lying on the floor,
blind drunk from politeness.

PATRICIA BEER

The Customer at the Ship Inn

This is the tavern that Sir Francis Drake
Always patronized in Exeter,

The menu says. Usually in luck,
And flush, in this Shippe out of water
He got annoyed only when clergymen
Declared that it stood in St Martin's Lane
And not Fysshe Street like everybody else.
He said you tend to get that near cathedrals.

I come here often too, red-veined and sprawling,
Stories quite good but rather repetitious.
The devil does not like this cheerful bawling
Under a low roof, and swings his vicious
Tail another way. All the king's men
Retreat as I can tell them to do when
Valium and alcohol and company
Conjure a brave person out of anxiety.

Reprieve is beautiful, although it can
Not pull down the scaffold. Up the wheel
Of the world the galleons begin
To swing, armed to the heart but dodgeable.
Massive and bright soon now they will appear.
No need for some bedraggled mariner
To sweat in with a warning from the coast
To say the might of Spain is on the seas
No need for anyone to write: 'I must
To Plimouth, and another ship than this.'

Jury Duty

'Harrods of Oxford Street'
The defendant says.
A mistake is a lie.

'I don't want to know'
The witness says.
So she does know.

'I swear by Almighty God'
Twelve of us say.
No lightning nowadays.

Four hours' talk at the police station
Has fitted into one page of notes.
What were they doing?

Someone has handled
A ratty old jacket
And a smeared TV set.
Someone else has pretended
For five minutes and ineptly
To be a policeman.

Why does defence counsel challenge me?
Do I look prim about cannabis?
Is it my diamond ring?
Am I old?

I go home every night
To handle, to impersonate.

Overseas Student

This year they have set us
Lady into Fox.
I know what a lady is,
Smell, timbre and sex,
But not the other word,
It does not exist here.
So far I have not dared
To open the book. Fear
Of what the lady faces
Is better in ignorance.
If she goes into tight-laces
Or falls into a trance,
It would be quite harmless,
But in this huge hot land
Where so much is formless
I feel I cannot stand
Reading of some machine
That sucks her in perhaps,
Some angel she becomes, some queen.

Possibly two strong lips
Will take her, but will she then
Be in the stomach or the heart
Of a heroic man?
Shall I ever be able to start?

Lemmings

Lemmings die every year. Over the cliff
They pour, hot blood into cold sea,
So that you half imagine steam
Will rise. They do not part company
At first, but spread out, a brown team
Like seaweed, undulant and tough.

Light changes, and the wind may veer
As they swim out and on. The sea
May become sleek or shrewish. Foam
May blind them or may let them see
The wet horizon. It takes time.
They do not die within an hour.

One by one they leave the air
And drown as individuals.
From minute to minute they blink out
Like aeroplanes or stars or gulls
Whose vanishing is never caught.
All in time will disappear.

And though their vitality
Does not look morbid enough
People call it suicide
Which it has some appearance of.
But it may well be that the mood
In which each year these lemmings die

Is nothing worse than restlessness,
The need to change and nothing else.
They have learnt this piece of strand
So thoroughly it now seems false.

They jump, thinking there is land
Beyond them, as indeed there is.

JEAN EARLE

The Roof

The roof of the opposite house is dear to me.
I feel some promise in the meeting of roof-line and sky,
The quiver, the intuition of a far country.

Whatever it is that broods where the line meets the clouds or the
    lifting blue –
Not longing. Not memory –
Some wild benevolence of light and time,
Nothing to do with the crossed cables or the sad chimney pots,
Speaking to me.

Often a pigeon will sit all night on the roof,
Resting between journeys he never planned.
I wake and think about him – the small shape
Harboured in that odd certainty – which comforts me also,
I cannot give it a name –
Of reassurance, reminder. 'You were here once.
This is how it will be.'

How what will be? And where is 'here'?
Mosses spread up the slates, change with the weather,
Green rounds, pads of sharp yellow with foxy hairs,
Flying minute pins and flowers, that no one looks for, it seems,
Nor ever remarks the pigeon, except me.

Our window is a small square. Plants hide traffic and passers-by,
In this room I listen to music, read, chatter to those who come
    and chatter to me
But do not consider how the roof opposite meets the sky.

I know it must be a very far country.

Times of Turn Round

How we lunged over the fields to kill what worked in us
The morning after the will was read!
Scores that had added up for years,
Taken to bed – to jolly meetings –
To yesterday's grave.

And as our feet stabbed through the felting dew,
Somebody found a mushroom.
We all stared at it in his hand – the tension melting
Into the haze, and we quartering
Each an unspoken territory.
Like the fierce walking crows
Around mid day and again before sundown.
Our backs were black as crows and our beaks bent
And our claws sunk in the misted grass
With revived kinship. Call it mushroom fever –
Christ in a velvet hat.

Nor did the mighty family things
Ever get said.

I remember, too,
A day without any strings to future or past.
Baby on hip, I gleaned the moor of whinberries,
Wild for their fragrant blood. That was a round day!
Sun yellow, then white, then glowing red –
A truce with life.

Now and again recalled, these deep catalysts
Rise and impact – starry – against the darker whole,
Easing my lips out of their shadowed bite,
Stiff now (for time has gone),
In a mislaid smile.

Nanternis

How long ago it is, since the big harebells
All the way to the farm and the talk there

About dead people. We two so living!
Hams in the rafters dripping – plop – sweet fat.

Home afterwards, with a lantern!
Wasn't it beautiful – flitting its crazy pink
Over the road, and the lonely soul at the mill
Turning aside from it, in to his owls.
'Whoo-whoo!' we mocked. Who? So long ago now,
We hardly remember who.

When we got back, young men
Round a late fire, singing.
Strong necks, dark eyes throwing sparks –
Their voices roaring
Songs we don't hear any more, lusty together.

The lantern extinguished,
The harebells in darkness
That had flushed pink under our mindless roselight.

Outsize harebells.
Silly old songs.

WENDY COPE

A Policeman's Lot (after W. S. Gilbert)

'The progress of any writer is marked by those moments when he manages to outwit his own inner police system'. Ted Hughes

Oh, once I was a policeman young and merry (young and merry)
Controlling crowds and fighting petty crime (petty crime)
But now I work on matters literary (litererry)
And I am growing old before my time ('fore my time).
No, the imagination of a writer (of a writer)
Is not the sort of beat a chap would choose (chap would choose)
And they've assigned me a prolific blighter ('lific blighter) –
I'm patrolling the unconscious of Ted Hughes.

It's not the sort of beat a chap would choose (chap would choose) –
Patrolling the unconscious of Ted Hughes.

All our leave was cancelled in the lambing season (lambing season)
When bitter winter froze the drinking trough (drinking trough)
For our commander stated with good reason (with good reason)
That that's the kind of thing that starts him off (starts him off).
But anything with four legs causes trouble (causes trouble) –
It's worse than organising several zoos (several zoos),
Not to mention mythic creatures in the rubble (in the rubble),
Patrolling the unconscious of Ted Hughes.

It's worse than organising several zoos (several zoos) –
Patrolling the unconscious of Ted Hughes.

Although it's disagreeable and stressful (bull and stressful)
Attempting to avert poetic thought ('etic thought)
I could boast of times when I have been successful (been successful)
And conspiring compound epithets were caught ('thets were caught).
But the poetry statistics in this sector (in this sector)
Are enough to make a copper turn to booze (turn to booze)
And I do not think I'll make it to inspector (to inspector)
Patrolling the unconscious of Ted Hughes.

It's enough to make a copper turn to booze (turn to booze) –
Patrolling the unconscious of Ted Hughes.

from *Strugnell's Sonnets*

I

The expense of spirits is a crying shame,
So is the cost of wine. What bard today
Can live like old Khayyám? It's not the same –
A loaf and Thou and Tesco's beaujolais.
I had this bird called Sharon, fond of gin –
Could knock back six or seven. At the price

I paid a high wage for each hour of sin
And that was why I only had her twice.
Then there was Tracy who drank rum and coke,
So beautiful I didn't mind at first
But love grows colder. Now some other bloke
Is subsidising Tracy and her thirst.
I need a woman, honest and sincere,
Who'll come across on half a pint of beer.

II

My glass shall not persuade me I'm senescent,
Nor that it's time to curb my virile hunger.
I'm still as randy as an adolescent
And didn't have much fun when I was younger.
Pursuing girls was hopeless with my looks
(I used to pick my spots and make them worse)
So I consoled myself by reading books –
Philosophy, pornography and verse.
For years I poured my unfulfilled desire
Into sad songs – and now, to my delight,
Find women love a bard, however dire,
And overlook my paunch because I write.
One doesn't need much literary skill
To be the Casanova of Tulse Hill.

ELMA MITCHELL

Late Fall

About the height of noon
The manless creatures come to take the sun.
This one we call a butterfly
Has landed on my hand, I don't know why.

Some warmth or texture or suspected sap
Inveigled it into this possible trap.

Top-heavy; ticklish; nourished on a weed;
Dotted and dashed with signals I can't read,

It comes in black, white, orange, blue and brown,
Topples a moment and settles blandly down.

Calm in the sun that made today its day.

Be off, you.
Do whatever it is you have to do,

I do not kill, nor spare, nor pardon.
There is no god walking in this garden.

Thoughts After Ruskin

Women reminded him of lilies and roses.
Me they remind rather of blood and soap,
Armed with a warm rag, assaulting noses,
Ears, neck, mouth and all the secret places·

Armed with a sharp knife, cutting up liver,
Holding hearts to bleed under a running tap,
Gutting and stuffing, pickling and preserving,
Scalding, blanching, broiling, pulverising,
– All the terrible chemistry of their kitchens.

Their distant husbands lean across mahogany
And delicately manipulate the market,
While safe at home, the tender and the gentle
Are killing tiny mice, dead snap by the neck,
Asphyxiating flies, evicting spiders,
Scrubbing, scouring aloud, disturbing cupboards,
Committing things to dustbins, twisting, wringing,
Wrists red and knuckles white and fingers puckered,
Pulpy, tepid. Steering screaming cleaners
Around the snags of furniture, they straighten
And haul out sheets from under the incontinent
And heavy old, stoop to importunate young,
Tugging, folding, tucking, zipping, buttoning,
Spooning in food, encouraging excretion,
Mopping up vomit, stabbing cloth with needles,
Contorting wool around their knitting needles,
Creating snug and comfy on their needles.

Their huge hands! their everywhere eyes! their voices
Raised to convey across the hullabaloo,
Their massive thighs and breasts dispensing comfort,
Their bloody passages and hairy crannies,
Their wombs that pocket a man upside down!

And when all's over, off with overalls,
Quickly consulting clocks, they go upstairs,
Sit and sigh a little, brushing hair,
And somehow find, in mirrors, colours, odours,
Their essences of lilies and of roses.

Instead of a Flag

Instead of a flag
She hung out herself
Streaming from the staff.
Windhaul, sunbeat.

More brilliant than bunting
She hung there sailing
One hand, one foot, holding,
One hand one foot flying.

She flapped and cracked in the gale
And pointed the wind
Away from all her dears.
She was brave and kind

And, at sunset, hauled down
And put in a bed
In a nice warm ward
Away from the wind

And well out of her mind.

SELIMA HILL

Below Hekla

I appear like a bird from nowhere.
I have a new name.
I am as clean as a whistle.
I beat the buttermilk in big white bowls
until it is smooth.
I wash the pearly plates under the tap,
and fifty canvas bumpers and fifty socks.
They drip in the sun
below grey mountains like the moon's.

Each night I lift the children
in their sleep and hold out
the china pot for them:
Wilt thu pissa, elskan,
pissa, pissa I whisper
as I tiptoe from bed to bed . . .
Around midnight,
I go to the geyser below Hekla
and bathe in the warm water.

I am a short fat English girl.
I am twenty-five mothers.
I lead my children in a line
across the heather to the church.
The father watches me
from his dark door.
He shakes his head,
and takes me by the hand:
Blessa thu, elskan, blessa thu!

And now, September,
dust is flying: the bus is here.
I am ready.
I am on my way to Reykjavik,
Leith, Liverpool . . .
The children of the Barnaheimilid

are running to the gate like hens.
Good-bye, blessa thu,
give our love to the Beatles, good-bye.

The Fowlers of the Marshes

Three thousand years ago
they were fowling in the marshes
around Thebes – men in knotted skirts
and tiered faience collars,
who avoided the brown crocodile,
and loved the ibis, which they stalked
with long striped cats on strings,
under the eye of Nut, the goddess of the sky.

My mother's hushed peculiar world's the same:
she haunts it like the fowlers of the marshes,
tiptoeing gaily into history, sustained by gods
as strange to me as Lady Nut, and Anubis,
the oracular, the jackal-masked.
When I meet her at the station, I say
Hello, Mum! and think *Hello, Thoth,*
This is the Weighing of the Heart.

ALISON BRACKENBURY

Medine in Turkey

'Today' said Hassan – through a mouthful of honey –
'A girl will come who speaks French.' There came
A girl with straight brown hair, her eyes
Flecked with gold, a stiller honey.
Her French was pure and soft. Her name
Was Medine. Her paid study
Ended when her father died.
'Maintenant – j'aide ma mère. Je lis.'

'Je lis Freud,' she ventured, bare feet firm
On the rug's blurred leaves. She lived next door.

Each house leads to a tiny yard
With a dusty tree; white chickens squirm
In favourite hollows. She never saw
France; she sat, this grave brown child
Ten years younger than myself, unmarried
Alight, in their cool best room. She smiled.

There is no answer. Scholarships?
France, too, has hot bored villages
With girls who read all afternoon.
The arranged husband, or their child's care
Will not close up that watchful face
Flecked by lace curtains, endless sun;
Unmoved, she listens for the place
Where the book closes, where the footsteps run.

Two Gardeners

Too far: I cannot reach them: only gardens.
And stories of the roughness of their lives.
The first, an archaeologist, had lost
Her husband to the Great War; never married
Again, but shared her fierce father's house;
Lit oil lamps and humped bright jugs of water
Until he died. We went there selling flags
Stopped at the drive's turn: silenced by her garden.

White water-lilies smoked across her pools.
The trees were hung with musk-roses
Pale as Himalayas; in darker space
Gleamed plants as tall as children, crowned with yellow,
Their name I never learnt. Her friends had found
Smuggled, her seeds, and lush stalks, from abroad;
While she walked with her father's snapping dog
Or drew the Saxon fields of Lincolnshire.

The other lived in the cold Northern side
Of a farmhouse, split for the farm's workers,
(Where we lived then). Once she had been a maid,

Had two children for love before she married
A quiet man. Away from her dark kitchen
She built a bank, her husband carried soil.
There she grew monkey flowers, red and yellow,
Brilliant as parrots, but more richly soft.
She said I could help plant them but I dare
Not touch the trembling petals – would not now.
I have sown some; I do not look to see
such generous gold and scarlet, on dark air.

Both live; I call them gardeners. And I grow
angry for them, that they might be called
typically English. They were no more that
Than sun or wind, were wild and of no place.
The roots of light plants touched them for a while
But could not hold them: when they moved
They left all plants to strangers

                            in whose dust
the suburbs' wind sucks up white petals round me
to look and see them in their earth-dark shoes
skirts stained by water, longer yet than ours.

Dazzled by dry streets I touch their hands,
parted by the sunlight, no man's flowers.

GWEN HARWOOD

David's Harp

Saturday morning. I rehearse
the Sunday hymns, fortissimo,
in the cool twilight of the church,
adding new stops at every verse.
Someone creaks the west door. I know
I am the object of his search,
gazed at, as though from far away;
he must be thirty if a day.

I turn my seventeen-year-old
profile a trifle heavenwards,
and hastily reduce the sound,
accommodating to his bold
descant on *David's Harp*. The Lord's
house might as well be Circe's ground.
  'With thee all night I mean to stay
  and wrestle till the break of day.'

'With thee all night.' So Wesley wrote,
though not with secular intent.
What flourishes that tune will bear.
My tenor wreathes it note by note
in rich Handelian ornament.
Faint burnt-out incense on the air
offends his Presbyterian nose.
He sneezes, stares across the rows

of empty pews between us; still
singing, walks to the organ; stands
beside me; puts his arms around
my waist and squeezes me until
I gasp, then gently lifts my hands
in his, and kisses me. He's sound
of wind. His kiss is long. We share
at last a common need for air.

'Give me one kiss, my bonnie lass!'
Vain as a cat, I frown and toss
my head. He watches Brisbane's hot
sunshine, strained through Victorian glass,
lacquer a Station of the Cross.
He scowls and thunders: 'Thou shalt not
make any graven images.'
But as he bends his head to kiss

the image of his hope, the door
moves with its useful warning creak.
He steps aside. I start to play.

He fills his lungs, and sings once more:
'Speak to me now, in mercy speak.'
A death-pale curate come to pray
kneels and is forced to find his Lord
through a loud F sharp major chord.

Where's that bright man who loved me when
there was not much to love? He died
soon after. The undying flow
of music bears him close again
handsome and young, while I am tried
in time's harsh fires. Dear man, I know
your worth, being now less ignorant of
the nature and the names of love.

The Sea Anemones

Grey mountains, sea and sky. Even the misty
sea wind is grey. I walk on lichened rock
in a kind of late assessment, call it peace.
Then the anemones, scarlet, gouts of blood.
There is a word I need, and earth was speaking.
I cannot hear. These sea-flowers are too bright.
Kneeling on rock, I touch them through cold water.
My fingers meet some hungering gentleness.
A newborn child's lips moved so, at my breast.
I woke once with my palm across your mouth.
   The word is: *ever*. Why add salt to salt?
   Blood drop by drop among the rocks they shine.
   Anemos, wind. The spirit, where it will.
   Not flowers, no, animals that must eat or die.

ANTIGONE KEFALA

The Place

   I
The place was small, full of hills,
palm trees, almond trees, oleanders,

glass flowers falling from the sky
on the ascetic hills, the bare houses.
The ancients had been there looking for copper.

Around the courtyards in the dusk
grey men in army coats
followed the leader round the ramparts.
At night after the toll, the three
would come dressed up to count the souls.

We waited there two summers.
Tall birds with upturned beaks
picked us like grain.
We moved in herds
waited with patience to be fed
drank at the water places
between the walls our necks grew longer
stretching for the night.

       II
The ships, we heard, had sunk
weighed with the charity of the new world
that kept on feeding us with toys
letters in foreign tongues
that we could not decipher.

We gave them to our silent children, onyx eyed,
brought up on wakes for spirits that had gone
and knew each drop that added the ingredients
to the day in the appointed measure.

For them, we looked at the crossroads
to find only the sound of running water
and the dusk settling in plum coloured
over the hills
the coolness of the evening full of promise.

       III
They came in spring with the great winds
the buyers
walked through the gates in groups

their marrow discoloured
their eyes ashes
gestures full of charity.

Bidders, in markets for flesh
untouched by the taste of the coffee
and the scent of the water
on the hot stones.

IV
We travelled in old ships
with small decaying hearts
rode on the giant beast
uncertain
remembered other voyages
and the black depths
each day we feasted on the past
friends watching over
the furniture of generations
dolphins no longer followed us
we were in alien waters.

JILL HELLYER

Living With Aunts

I
Passed to two maiden aunts, the quiet child
absorbed the trinity of their beliefs;
only in adolescence she learned to cry
and later, much later, to analyse her griefs.

Her thoughts were tracts they never visited:
the child became myself, always unknown
but present, obedient, silent. I watched them eat
slowly, talk slowly, and the seeds were sown

of the divinity of the *Sydney Morning Herald*,
the British Empire, and the ABC:

I was always told how fortunate I was
as though my needs were met by literacy.

My aunt once saw reviewed in her Saturday *Herald*
The Rise and Fall of the British Empire. She
read it to us in helpless disbelief.
(It wasn't mentioned on the ABC)

2

I'd always thought Soames Forsyte was a cousin,
I'd heard so much about him. One aunt read
all of the Saga, the other had poor eyesight
so she and I both painstakingly were fed

news of the Forsytes slowly at the table.
I knew Soames better than I knew my father
whose death I learned about in secret from
a *Herald* clipping. I was the child left over.

3

I was always a bother to them, and they'd say
You're not a proper Hellyer, not with brown eyes
(as though it were a crime). I was the wrong
dreamer of wrong dreams, was the wrong size,

never came first in the class for them nor brandished
my energy for causes they considered noble.
But the British Empire after all had fallen
too while they ate so slowly at the table.

DOROTHY HEWETT

Legend of the Green Country

I

September is the spring month bringing tides, swilling green in
    the harbour mouth,
Turnabout dolphins rolling-backed in the rip and run, the king
    waves

Swinging the coast, snatching at fishermen from Leeuwin to
  Norah's Head;
A dangerous month: but I count on an abacus as befits a
  shopkeeper's daughter.
I never could keep count by modern methods, the ring of the till
Is profit and loss, the ledger, hasped with gold, sits in its heavy
  dust
On the counter, out front the shopkeeper's sign hangs loose and
  bangs in the wind,
The name is obliterated, the dog swells and stinks in the gutter,
The golden smell of the beer does not run in the one street, like
  water,
The windmill head hangs, broken-necked, flapping like a great
  plain turkey
As the wind rises . . . this was my country, here I go back for
  nurture
To the dry soaks, to the creeks running salt through the timber,
To the ghosts of the sandalwood cutters, and the blue breath of
  their fires,
To the navvies in dark blue singlets laying rails in the scrub.

My grandfather rode out, sawing at a hard-mouthed ginger
  horse,
And a hard heart in him, a dray full of rum and beer, bully-beef
  and treacle,
Flour and tea, workboots and wideawakes with the corks
  bobbing for flies;
Counting the campfires in the dusk, counting the men, counting
  the money,
Counting the sheep from the goats, and the rack-rented railway
  houses.
No wonder I cannot count for the sound of the money-changers,
The sweat and the clink, the land falling into the cash register,
Raped and eroded, thin and black as a myall girl on a railway
  siding.
He came back, roaring and singing up from the gullies, his beard
Smelt of rum, his money-bag plump as a wild duck under his
  saddle.

The old horse stumbled in the creek-bed but brought him home,
The dray rattled; as they took him down in the yard he cursed
and swore
At the dream, and blubbered for it: next Saturday night he rode
his horse
Up the turkey red carpet into the bar, smashing the bottles and
glasses,
Tipping the counter, sending the barmaid screaming, her breasts
tilting with joy.
The great horse reared and he sang and swore and flung his hat
at the sky,
And won his bets, and rode home, satisfied, to a nagging wife
and daughter,
Having buried his pain and his lust under the broken bottles.
The publican swept them up in the cold light next morning,
And that was the end of it, they thought, but it wasn't so easy:
There is no end to it and I stand at the mole watching the sea
run out,
Or hang over the rails at the Horseshoe Bridge and listen to the
tide,
Listen to the earth that pleasured my grandfather with his flocks
and acres
Drowned under salt, his orange trees forked bare as unbreeched
boys.
Only the apples, little and hard, bitten green and bitter as salt,
They come up in the spring, in the dead orchard they are the
fruit
Of our knowledge, and I am Eve, spitting the pips in the eye of
the myth-makers.
This is my legend; an old man on a ginger horse who filled his
till
And died content with a desert, or so they said: his stone angel
Cost a pretty penny, but the workmanship was faulty, its wings
curve
In a great arc over the graveyard, it grows mildewed and dirty,
Its nose is syphilitic, its feet splay like a peasant, its hands
Clasp over its breast like the barmaid who screamed in the pub,
And kissed him, for love, not money, but only once.

II

My grandmother had a bite like a sour green apple,
Little and pitiless she kept the till,
Counted the profits, and stacked the bills of sale.
She bought the shops and the farms, the deeds were hers,
In the locked iron safe with a shower of golden sovereigns.
She never trusted the banks, they failed in the nineties,
She kept her bank notes rolled in the top of her stocking,
Caressingly, while her prices soared and dropped,
Her barometer; crops and wool and railway lines.
Each night she read the news by the hurricane lantern,
While the only child wept for love in the washing-up water.
She could argue like a man, politics, finance, banking.
In her rocking chair with her little dangling feet,
Her eyes glittered like broken beer bottle glass.
She kept one eye out for a farmer to spend his money
And a sharp tongue for a borrowing mate of my grandfather's.

Once, long ago, in Swanston Street she 'made'
For fashionable ladies, their breasts half bared
And their ankles covered, pads in their hair,
Bustles, bugle beads and jet, dyed ostrich feathers,
You could see their shadows waving from hansom cabs,
And the ghostly wheels turning into Swanston Street.
She had her miracles and quoted them . . .
Science and Health by Mary Baker Eddy,
She read *The Monitor* while the dust storms whirled,
And marvelled that God was love; it was all clear profit.
She wet the bagging to filter the westerlies,
Planted geraniums and snowdrops under the tank,
And squashed black caterpillars on moonlit forays.
She balanced the ledger and murmured, 'God is love',
Feeling like God, she foreclosed on another farm.

She never read for pleasure, or danced or sang,
Or listened with love, slowly life smote her dumb,
Till she lay in the best bedroom, pleating the quilt,
In a fantasy of ball dresses for Melbourne ladies.

Her eyes were remote as pennies, her sheets stank,
She cackled and counted a mythical till all her days.

III

My father was a black-browed man who rode like an Abo.
The neighbors gossiped, 'A touch of the tarbrush there.'
He built the farm with his sweat, it lay in the elbow
Of two creeks, thick with wattle and white ti-tree.
At night he blew on the cornet; once, long ago, he'd played
On the pleasure cruises that went up the Yarra on Saturday
    nights;
The lights bobbed in the muddy water, the girls in white muslin
    sang 'Tipperary'.
Now he played in the lonely sleepout, looking out over the flat,
With the smell of creekwater, and a curlew crying like a
    murdered gin,
Crying all night, till he went out with a shotgun and finished its
    screaming,
But not his own . . . he, the mendicant, married the store-
    keeper's daughter.

My mother was a dark round girl in a country town,
With down on her lip, her white cambric blouse
Smelt of roses and starch, she was beautiful,
Warm, and frigid in a world of dried-up women,
Aborting themselves with knitting needles on farms.
She wept in the tin humpy at the back of the store,
For the mother who hated, the father who drank
And loved her; then, sadly, she fell in love
And kissed the young accountant who kept the books,
Behind the ledgers, the summer dust on the counters.
He was on the booze, broke all his promises,
Went off to the city and sang in an old spring cart,
'Bottle-oh, Bottle-oh' till his liver gave out
And he died; she married in arum lilies, satin, tulle,
Under the bell that tolled for the storekeeper's daughter.
Men shot themselves in the scrub on her wedding day.
My father brought her wildflowers, rode forty miles,

But he never kissed her like the beautiful bottle-oh,
Boozing in the pub like a fly caught in its amber.

The roof of the hospital cracked like purgatory,
At sunset the birth blood dried on the sheets,
Nobody came to change them, the sun went down,
The pain fell on her body like a beast and mauled it.

She hated the farm, hated the line of wattles
Smudging the creek, kept her hands full of scones,
Boiled the copper, washing out sins in creek water,
Kept sex at bay like the black snake coiled in the garden,
Burning under the African daisies and bridal creeper,
Took her children to bed, he lay alone in the sleep-out,
With a headache and *The Seven Pillars of Wisdom*.
The girls in their picture hats came giggling and singing,
Trailing their hands like willows from the Yarra launches,
Till the dream was nightmare and all his life a regret,
Bought and gelded in an old grey house by a creek-bed.

IV

My grandfather rode round the sheep in leggings, and fed the
    calves,
He mended the gates, once a month he drove into town to his
    'lodge',
A white carnation picked at dusk from my grandmother's
    garden,
A dress suit with a gold watch, a chain looped over his belly,
Magnificent! . . . but my father only grinned sourly and read
    Remarque's
All Quiet on the Western Front, while my mother polished his
    medals
For Anzac Day. They never understood him, none of the
    shopkeepers' breed,
Christ! how could they? They only had a copy of the Bible,
My grandmother quoted it (mostly wrong), and Tennyson bound
    in morocco,
'The Stag at Bay' on the sitting room wall, two elephants from
    Bombay,

Spoil from the trip they took 'home' . . . was it a century ago?
The piano where, once a year, we sang hymns, when the minister
    came.
They had no religion, they believed in themselves, no other,
Self-made men and women who sat round their groaning table,
While all the no-hopers were taken over by the banks,
Or walked off, and took up dead-end jobs in the city;
The farms lay at their boundaries breeding dust and rabbits.
They breasted it all, the waves of drought and depression,
Of flood and fire, sown in sparks from the black steam trains
Roaring through wheat and the dead white grass by the sidings.
Their haystacks burnt as gold as their money bags, their till
Was full of horses drooling on oats and rock salt, of cows
With udders streaming white milk in the frosty mornings,
Of roosters crowing their triumph from the stable roof, and
    orchards,
Green as their hopes, tangy with peach, cradled with quail and
    oranges.
Only the sheep bleating their thin cry on the winter evenings,
Echoed the crows, the scavengers that were our kinsmen.
The woolly ghosts cropped the grass to its roots; the hard hoofs
Beat a track to the end of a world where the creeks ran dry,
The lambs lay blind while the crows ate their eyes in the salmon
    gums,
And the timberless paddocks blew in dust as far as the sea.

V

Only the man with the cornet, who rode with Remarque
Across his saddle bows, only he loved the soil,
Running it through his fingers he sensed its dying,
Its blowing away on the winds of time and cut timber,
He saw the salt of its death rising.
He said, 'I have a plan', and rode with it into the cities,
A plan for trees, acres of trees blowing by creekbeds,
Forests marching in long green lines to save a country,
Picking up their roots and digging them into the earth,
Holding it fast against the salt and the wind tides.
But the laughter rose in gales from the men in cities,

Their desks shook, their papers scattered like almond blossom in
   storm,
'Visionary' . . . 'Dreamer . . . go back to the bend in two creeks,
Thick with wattle and ti-tree you have grown to love,
Go back and wait for the trees to wither, the creek to run,
Drowned in salt, for this is your heritage . . .'
'Years from now we will not be sitting here, we will be gone',
And where will you go, man the great Dreamer . . . dead and the
   land dead,
Only your ghost will ride like an Abo, crying 'Trees' through the
   corrugated iron
Of the sidings, where the rails buckle with heat and men sit
   smoking
And brooding on a green world, as you once dreamed of
   Gippsland,
Under the fern-choked water, falling, falling: you tried to give us
A vision of greenness and water, who were bred out of desert
   and scrub
And sheep crying and crow . . . our father whispered 'Trees' as
   he blew 'Tipperary'.

VI
The women were strong and they destroyed the men,
Lying locked and cold in their sexless beds,
Putting greed in their men's fingers instead of love.
They drove them from the earth, left them derelict,
Dead mutton hanging on hooks on the verandahs.
For them the curlew wailed, the old horse lay
Trapped in the paddock all night with rheumaticky haunches.
My grandfather wept, 'Whoa back there Ginger, whoa back,'
Till the glasses winked in the bar like barmaids' eyes,
The virgins in muslin, the pretty French girls from Marseilles,
And a little whore in the rain on Princess Bridge.
Where would they go, rich, gelded and blind,
Tugging their old mad women with them to their graves?

VII
This land is not mine to give or trade,
I have no lien on these sad acres,

Where the crow flies home,
A solitary reaper.
The milky creek runs death,
The wattle and the ti-tree are all gone.
My father went, exiled himself in cities,
Sour as a green apple, his tap-root broken.

The orchard lies a nameless graveyard
Behind the farm, stripped of its flowers and fruit,
Its trees, its birds, its bees murmuring.
Only the skull of a sheep dropped at the cross-roads,
And the rattling dray in the scrub on the empty skyline,
My grandfather yelling, 'Whoa back there Ginger, whoa back.
While I carry my money bags home through the heart of this
    country.'
The wheels of the old dray turning, bring us full circle,
Death whirls in the wind, the old house hunches in on itself
And sleeps like the blind, 'The Stag at Bay' hangs skewed
On the wall, the elephants from Bombay are chipped by the
    children,
Nobody plays 'Rock of Ages' on the untuned piano now.
But the crows cry over my salty acres, scavengers come home
To roost and foul their nests in the creaking gum trees.

VIII

Who rises from the dead each spring must pay the cost.
How shall I pay living at the harbour's mouth
Where my father's ghost sits mumbling over breakfast,
Nodding at headlines, full of strikes and wool boards,
Tariffs to sink his teeth into, wars for his grandsons,
Where's Remarque now! His medals on the wall blink
Their derision, his heart's grown crooked, out of season.
He forgets how to sink a well or plant a tree.
His back's like sandalwood, his smell is sweet with death.
He crumbles where he sits, the tide rises to his lips.
Mother to daughter the curse drops like a stone.
My mother sits silent with nothing to remember.

Yet sometimes in the dark I come upon him in his chair,
A book lying open on his knees, his eye turned inward,
And then he sings old songs of Bendigo and windlasses,
And tells me tales of Newport railway workers, Nellie Melba
Singing High Mass, and how he read all night in Collingwood,
Voted for Labor and fell in love with Nellie Stewart.
But never a word of that far green country of his spirit,
Where the trees grow greener than the Gippsland grass.
All this is locked away in grief and salt.
Maybe, in death, his lips will whisper it,
And the green vision that gave sap to all his days
Will rise again and give him back his country.

    IX
This is *my* truth, a grandfather boozed with guilt
And gold, who got free kisses from a barmaid for his gift,
And a great horse that swung its rump and tilted the world
    down.
A man rides through the windmill country like an Abo,
Blowing his cornet in a wail of 'Trees', bewitched
By Gippsland fern and luminous girls mirrored in the Yarra.
I will pay this debt, go back and find my place,
Pick windfalls out of the grass like a mendicant.
The little sour apples still grow in my heart's orchard,
Bitten with grief, coming up out of the dead country.
Here I will eat their salt and speak my truth.

ANNA SWIRSZCZYNSKA

Tr. Margaret Marshment and Grazyra Baran

She Can't Sleep

At night the girl
sits curled up on the bed.
She looks at the boy
who sleeps beside her.

At night the girl
sits curled up on the bed.
She looks at the window.
Not long till dawn.

He Treats them to Ice-cream

Every Sunday they went for a walk together.
He, she
and the three children.

One night
when she tried to stop him going
to his other woman,
he pulled out a flick-knife
from under the mattress.

They still go for a walk
every Sunday,
he, she and the three children.
He treats them to ice-cream and they all laugh.
She too.

Peasant Woman

She carries on her shoulders
the house, the garden, the farm,
the cows, the pigs, the calves, and the children.

Her back wonders
why it doesn't break.
Her hands wonder
why they don't fall off.
She doesn't wonder.

Like a bloodstained stick
her dead mother's drudgery
sustains her.
They used the lash
on her great-grandmother.

That lash
shines on her through the clouds
instead of the sun.

Family Life

He goes for her
with his fists.

He flicked off
like a fly from his breeches
the two small hands
that try to stop him.

Two Old Women

The two of us sit in the doorway,
chatting about our children and grandchildren.
We sink happily
into our oldwomanhood.

Like two spoons
sinking
into a bowl of hot porridge.

The Reaper

Fat like the sun,
panting in the sun,
she hurls into the panting threshing-machine
the panting suns
of sheaves.

Her Greatest Love

At sixty she's experiencing
the greatest love of her life.

She walks arm in arm with her lover,
the wind ruffles their grey hairs.

Her lover says:
— You have hair like pearls.

Her children say:
— You silly old fool.

ASTRIDE IVASKA

Tr. Inara Cedrins

To the Memory of a Poet

This spring the cuckoo won't count out your years,
Naomi, nor will the Rain King invite you
to walk over the sea, patting wave-backs.
This spring we will leave you
in your green-glass palace,
alone behind many blind windows.
Your radiance will unfurl
around blossoming chokecherry branches,
and you'll no longer fear
tide nor ebb,
nor the moon's changing moods.
We won't tell you about the festivities
for which we were so solemnly preparing,
when we came upon you—trodden bloom,
sprig of lemon verbena on the garden walk.
As a broken sunflower we found you,
Naomi, and we wrapped you up
in the Rain King's veils,
asking in whispers
what sort of wasteful creator is he,
who left you on the garden walk.
We placed chokecherry flowers
over your light-grey eyes,
and forbade the cuckoo to call,
so that you might dream, Naomi,
of your life's miraculous chance.

That Which has Remained Unlived
to the Memory of a Poet

That which has remained unlived,
in this world unlived,
will hurt in the next.

      Cloudberries ripen in the marshes.

That which has remained unsown,
in this world unsown,
will wither in the next.

      I have no basket.

That which has remained unsaid,
in this world unspoken,
will weep in the next.

      Cloudberries freeze in ice.

ANA BLANDIANA

Tr. Michael Impey

Links

I myself am everything.
Find me a leaf that bears no resemblance,
Help me find an animal
Which doesn't groan with my voice.
Wherever I tread the earth cracks
And the dead that bear my likeness
I see embracing and procreating other dead.
Why so many links with the world,
So many parents and unnatural descendants
And all this crazy resembling?
The universe haunts me with thousands of my faces
And my only defense is to strike myself.

GABRIELA MELINESCU

Tr. W. B. and Matei Calinescu

Birth

Let us bring out those heavy dice
cut from elephant tusks.
Let us hammer them on the wet earth
till under the pounding they crack.
And good luck bursts out.
No one knows how it looks:
maybe it's a horrible beast
or steam hovering over neverness.
I sit on my knees. I illumine
the uncertain birth from ivory,
and elephants come squealing.
They hold up my temples with their tusks.

NATALYA GORBANEVSKAYA

Tr. Daniel Weissbort

'Wipe the bliss . . .'

Wipe the bliss of half-sleep from your cheeks
and open your eyes wide until the lids ache,
the filth and whiteness of the ward
is like the voluntary flag of your bondage.

The emptiness and narrowness of the ward –
close your eyes tightly until your cheeks ache.
Wipe the smile off your chapped lips,
but swallow the ineffectual scream.

The half-dark, half-light of the ward –
and your neighbour, with closed eyes,
insensibly cursing the white light,
soundlessly dissolves in tears.

Three Poems on the Road

1

Early morning,
Petersburg dark,
I am going to Yurev
on Saint Yury's day.

Blue morning,
the sun in its grave,
To test my fate
I wander the world.

Under the lamps
it's still not bright,
I go underground
in Brodsky Street.

2

But I preferred the whirlpools of Decembrism
to Kuchel's Derpt,
that safe moorage was
too close to Petersburg.

No, better to roam half Europe,
to risk one's life
at the hands of a hired killer
and, returning to one's native land,
to wind oneself about with iron shackles
as with a gentle shroud.

3

to G. Kornilovaya

Lord, we all of us seek salvation,
seek it in every nook and cranny.
I shall stand on the Narva road like a candle
and vote for the lorries.

Do I know where I shall be tomorrow,
Tartu or Vorkuta – do I know,

a truck, majestic as a brontosaurus,
keeps its wheels turning.

Who is up there, invisible, above me?
A cherub's face is spotlit.
Darling, do not pass me by,
or everything will vanish in the smoke.
The roads do not lead to Rome
but from Rome, ever further.

'And you . . .'

And you, candle, determined I
must be a holder for your eyes, your wax,
that in the pitch black everlasting night,
your trembling flame alone should gaze into the dark.

But the sill is a frontier to candlelight,
the curtain's swaying is your Boreas,
and where is the fire-worshipper more secure
than in November behind double windows.

I am not a flame, not a candle, but a light,
I am a fire-fly in the damp, tangled
grass. The grass flows swiftly after me
and the woodland beast homes on me in silence: –

The faintest of brightening fire-flies,
the brightest of failing fire-flies,
by whose light the night skies are not pierced,
yet the stars are guided in their courses.

'Something's with me . . .'

Something's with me, something
or almost nothing.
I enter my being
like a plane going into a spin.

I strip off my skin
like a coat – serenely.

Someone's with me, somebody,
a certain one, no one.

BELLA AKHMADULINA

Tr. Elaine Feinstein

Fever

I must be ill, of course. I've been shivering
for three days now like a horse before the races.
Even the haughty man who lives on my landing
has said as much to me:
Bella, you're shaking!

Please control yourself, this strange disease of yours
is rocking the walls, it gets in everywhere.
My children are driven mad by it, and at night
it shatters all my cups and kitchenware.

I tried to answer him: Yes,
I do tremble,
more and more, though I mean no harm to anyone.
But tell everyone on the floor, in any case,
I've made up my mind to leave the house this evening.

However, I was then so jerked about by
fever, my words shook with it; my legs
wobbled; I couldn't even bring my
lips together into the shape of a smile.

My neighbour, leaning over the banister,
observed me with disgust he didn't hide.
Which I encouraged.
– This is just
a beginning. What happens next, I wonder.

Because this is no ordinary illness. I'm sorry to
tell you, there are as many wild and
alien creatures flashing about in me
as in a drop of water under a microscope.

My fever lashed me harder and harder, and
drove its sharp nails under my skin. It was
something like the rain whipping an
aspen tree, and damaging every leaf.

I thought: I seem to be moving about rapidly
as I stand here, at least my muscles are moving.
My body is out of my control completely.
The thing is freely doing whatever it likes.

And it's getting away from me. I wonder if
it will suddenly and dangerously disappear?
Like a ball slipping out of a child's hand,
or a piece of string unreeling from a finger?

I didn't like any of it. To
the doctor
I said (though I'm timid with him)
– you know, I'm a proud woman! I can't have my
body disobeying me for ever!

My doctor explained:
Yours is a simple disease,
perhaps even harmless, unfortunately
you are vibrating so fast I can't examine you.

You see, when anything vibrates, as you are,
and its movements are so very quick and small,
the object is reduced, visibly speaking
to – nothing. All I can see is: mist.

So my doctor put his golden instrument
against my indefinite body, and a sharp
electric wave chilled me at once
as if I had been flooded with green fire

and the needle and the scales registered horror.
The mercury began to seethe with violence.
The glass shattered, everything splashed about,
and a few splinters drew blood from my fingers.

– Be careful, doctor, I cried. But
he wasn't worried.

Instead, he proclaimed: Your
poor organism is
now functioning normally.

Which made me sad. I knew myself to belong
to another norm than he had ever intended.
One that floated above my own spirit only
because I was too narrow for such immensity.

And those many figures of my ordeals had
trained my nervous system so that now
my nerves were bursting through my skin, like old
springs through a mattress, screeching at me.

My wrist was still out of shape with its huge
and buzzing pulse, that always had insisted
on racing greedily: Damn it then, run free, I cried
I'll choke with you, as Neva chokes St Petersburg.

For at night my brain has become so sharp with
waiting, my ear so open to silence, if
a door squeaks or a book drops, then –
with an explosion – it's the end of me.

I have never learnt to tame those beasts
inside, that guzzle human blood.
In my presence, draughts blow under doors!
Candles flare – before I extinguish them!

And one enormous tear is always ready
to spill over the rim of my eyes.
My own spirit distorts everything.
My own hell would corrupt heaven.

The doctor wrote me out a Latin scrip.
The sensible and healthy girl in
the chemist's shop was able to read the
music in it from the punctuation.

And now my whole house has been softened by
the healing kiss of that valerian,
the medicine has licked into every
wound I have, with its minty tongue.

My neighbour is delighted, three times he
has congratulated me on my recovery,
(through his children). He has even
put in a word for me with the house management.

I have repaid a few visits and debts already,
answered some letters. I wander about
in some kind of profitable circles.
And no longer keep any wine in my cupboard.

Around me – not a sound, not a soul.
My table is dead, dust hides everything on it.
My blunt pencils like illiterate
snouts, are all lying in darkness.

And like a defeated horse, all my
steps are sluggish and hobbling now.
So all is well. But my nights are
disturbed with certain dangerous premonitions.

My doctor has not yet found me out. However
it will not long be possible to
fool him. He may have cured me once, but
soon I know I shall burn and freeze again.

A snail in its grave of bone I am
for the moment saved by blindness and silence –
but still the horns of sick antennae itch
and will rise up once again from my forehead.

Star-fall of full stops and hyphens, I
summon your shower to me! I want to
die with the silvery goose-flesh of
water nymphs burning in my spine.

Fever! I am your tambourine, strike me
without pity! I shall dance, like

a ballerina to your music, or
live like a chilled puppy in your frost.

So far I haven't even begun to
shiver. No, let's not even discuss that. Yet
my observant neighbour is already
becoming rather cold to me when we meet.

Small Aircraft
Tr. Daniel Halpern

As if I didn't have enough
Bothering me, now I'm confused
By dreaming nightly
Of small airplanes. I don't understand it.

The planes don't care that I dream of them:
Now like chickens they peck seed
From my hand. Now like termites
They live in the walls of my house.

Or else they poke me
With their dumb noses: little fish
Move like this to a child's foot,
Tickling, making their feet laugh.

Sometimes they push and bump each other
Around my fire, blinded by the light.
They won't let me read and the noise
Of their wings excites me.

They have another trick: they come
To me like children in tears
And sit in my lap,
Crying, *Take us in your arms.*

You can drive them away, but they're right back,
Flying out of the polished darkness,
Looking from their eyes like sad dachshunds
As their long bodies float by.

YUNNA MORITZ

Tr. Elaine Feinstein

Midday in Gantiadi

His eyelids are dark as coffee, the Southerner,
who has taken pancakes stuffed with lamb from
the hot meat dish in the cauldron,
and the sexual charm in his smile is
as calm as the life of a vegetable
or the brown flesh of Greek olives.

He draws me secretly towards him, as if
by oil of camphor-wood, or some
insidious attraction without name,
older than the power of any reptile
and more abrupt than a pirate attack,
as if he was marked out in metal for me.

It is wrong to evade what you know,
as black ravens do if their path
should happen to cross the path of a bat;
forget your finicky pretence
of working miracles, though you long for them,
and always go to sleep in their light,

because you will wake again in idleness
and not be morally outraged, your spirit has
already been initiated.
Drink the Muscatel, gulp down
its fragrance from your chipped cylinder.
And for your sin? – hope only for forgiveness!

'Now we'll go'

Now we'll go homeward
   in search of a bed
in a silver pillar of
   Christmas snow

and there with one toe
  push the heel of the other
and so take our boots off
  without any bother:

then inside the coffee pot
  some strange drink rustles.
We are reminded
  how no soul is bounded;

and no talent can be
  a convenient mixture
of things that we like only:
  but what is best and what is worst.

NOVELLA MATVEYEVA

Tr. Daniel Weissbort

The Eggplants have Pins and Needles

The eggplants have pins and needles.
Long dreams have plagued their sleep.
By the redbrick garden wall
Cucumbers droop like whips.
The poppylamps blow out in the wind.
Petals flock the air and settle
Like colored reflections.
The sun, like sea-drowned amber, peers
Through a dense silt of cloud.
But nettles go on being nettles
And roosters go on being roosters.
Listen! A stubborn beating of wings!
One bird, well-advanced in years,
Feeling the winter coming on,
Plucks up his courage and lets forth,
But has clean forgotten the song,
The words, and the rasping sound
Sticks in his gullet.

The rooster stiffens,
Clenches his pale yellow foot.
Fatigue and rheumatic pain overwhelm him,
As winter wags its blanched finger.
His plumage flutters somberly,
Like a fire behind bars.
His comb glows like elderberry.
His feathers gleam,
Rheumatically mossed,
And the rooster's faint shadow
Smells distinctly of the cold.

MARIANNE MOORE

The Mind, Intractable Thing

even with its own ax to grind, sometimes
   helps others. Why can't it help me?

     O imagnifico,
wizard in words – poet, was it, as
Alfredo Panzini defined you?
Weren't you refracting just now
on my eye's half-closed triptych
   the image, enhanced, of a glen –
'the foxgrape festoon as sere leaves fell'
on the sand-pale dark byroad, one leaf adrift
   from the thin-twigged persimmon; again,

     a bird – Arizona
caught-up-with, uncatchable cuckoo
after two hours' pursuit, zigzagging
road-runner, stenciled in black
stripes all over, the tail
   windmilling up to defy me?
You understand terror, know how to deal
with pent-up emotion, a ballad, witchcraft.
   I don't. O Zeus and O Destiny!

Unafraid of what's done,
undeterred by apparent defeat,
you, imagnifico, unafraid
of disparagers, death, dejection,
have out-wiled the Mermaid of Zennor,
    made wordcraft irresistible:
reef, wreck, lost lad, and 'sea-foundered bell' –
as near a thing as we have to a king –
    craft with which I don't know how to deal.

Dream

After coming on Jerome S. Shipman's comment concerning academic appointments for artists.

    The committee – now a permanent body –
        formed to do but one thing,
discover positions for artists, was worried, then happy;
rejoiced to have magnetized Bach and his family
    'to Northwestern,' besides five harpsichords
        without which he would not leave home.
For his methodic unmetronomic melodic diversity
contrapuntally appointedly persistently
        irresistibly Fate-like Bach – find me words.

Expected to create for university
        occasions, inventions with wing,
was no trouble after master-classes (stiffer in Germany),

each week a cantata; chorales, fugues, concerti!
    Here, students, craved a teacher and each student worked.
    Jubilation! Re-joicings! Felicity!
    Repeated fugue-like, all of it, to infinity.
    (Note too that over-worked Bach was not irked.)

Haydn, when he had heard of Bach's billowing sail,
begged Prince Esterházy to lend him to Yale.
Master-mode expert fugue-al forms since, prevail.

Dazzling nonsense . . . I imagine it? Ah! nach
enough. J. Sebastian – born at Eisenach:
its coat-of-arms in my dream: BACH PLAYS BACH!

Enough

1969

Am I a fanatic? The opposite.
    And where would I like to be?
    Sitting under Plato's olive tree
or propped against its thick old trunk,

        away from controversy
        or anyone choleric.

If you would see stones set right, unthreatened
    by mortar (masons say 'mud'),
    squared and smooth, let them rise as they should,
Ben Jonson said, or he implied.

        In 'Discoveries' he then said,
        'Stand for truth. It's enough.'

ELIZABETH BISHOP

The Moose
For Grace Bulmer Bowers

From narrow provinces
of fish and bread and tea,
home of the long tides
where the bay leaves the sea
twice a day and takes
the herrings long rides,

where if the river
enters or retreats
in a wall of brown foam
depends on if it meets

the bay coming in,
the bay not at home;

where, silted red,
sometimes the sun sets
facing a red sea,
and others, veins the flats'
lavender, rich mud
in burning rivulets;

on red, gravelly roads,
down rows of sugar maples,
past clapboard farmhouses
and neat, clapboard churches,
bleached, ridged as clamshells,
past twin silver birches,

through late afternoon
a bus journeys west,
the windshield flashing pink,
pink glancing off of metal,
brushing the dented flank
of blue, beat-up enamel;

down hollows, up rises,
and waits, patient, while
a lone traveller gives
kisses and embraces
to seven relatives
and a collie supervises.

Goodbye to the elms,
to the farm, to the dog.
The bus starts. The light
grows richer; the fog,
shifting, salty, thin,
comes closing in.

Its cold, round crystals
form and slide and settle
in the white hens' feathers,

in gray glazed cabbages,
on the cabbage roses
and lupins like apostles;

the sweet peas cling
to their wet white string
on the whitewashed fences;
bumblebees creep
inside the foxgloves,
and evening commences.

One stop at Bass River.
Then the Economies –
Lower, Middle, Upper;
Five Islands, Five Houses,
where a woman shakes a tablecloth
out after supper.

A pale flickering. Gone.
The Tantramar marshes
and the smell of salt hay.
An iron bridge trembles
and a loose plank rattles
but doesn't give way.

On the left, a red light
swims through the dark:
a ship's port lantern.
Two rubber boots show,
illuminated, solemn.
A dog gives one bark.

A woman climbs in
with two market bags,
brisk, freckled, elderly.
'A grand night. Yes, sir,
all the way to Boston.'
She regards us amicably.

Moonlight as we enter
the New Brunswick woods,

hairy, scratchy, splintery;
moonlight and mist
caught in them like lamb's wool
on bushes in a pasture.

The passengers lie back.
Snores. Some long sighs.
A dreamy divagation
begins in the night,
a gentle, auditory,
slow hallucination . . .

In the creakings and noises,
an old conversation
— not concerning us,
but recognizable, somewhere,
back in the bus:
Grandparents' voices

uninterruptedly
talking, in Eternity:
names being mentioned,
things cleared up finally;
what he said, what she said,
who got pensioned;

deaths, deaths and sicknesses;
the year he remarried;
the year (something) happened.
She died in childbirth.
That was the son lost
when the schooner foundered.

He took to drink. Yes.
She went to the bad.
When Amos began to pray
even in the store and
finally the family had
to put him away.

'Yes . . .' that peculiar
affirmative. 'Yes . . .'
A sharp, indrawn breath,
half groan, half acceptance,
that means 'Life's like that.
We know *it* (also death).'

Talking the way they talked
in the old featherbed,
peacefully, on and on,
dim lamplight in the hall,
down in the kitchen, the dog
tucked in her shawl.

Now, it's all right now
even to fall asleep
just as on all those nights.
– Suddenly the bus driver
stops with a jolt,
turns off his lights.

A moose has come out of
the impenetrable wood
and stands there, looms, rather,
in the middle of the road.
It approaches; it sniffs at
the bus's hot hood.

Towering, antlerless,
high as a church,
homely as a house
(or, safe as houses).
A man's voice assures us
'Perfectly harmless . . .'

Some of the passengers
exclaim in whispers,
childishly, softly,
'Sure are big creatures.'

'It's awful plain.'
'Look! It's a she!'

Taking her time,
she looks the bus over,
grand, otherworldly.
Why, why do we feel
(we all feel) this sweet
sensation of joy?

'Curious creatures,'
says our quiet driver,
rolling his *r*'s.
'Look at that, would you.'
Then he shifts gears.
For a moment longer,

by craning backward,
the moose can be seen
on the moonlit macadam;
then there's a dim
smell of moose, an acrid
smell of gasoline.

One Art

The art of losing isn't hard to master;
so many things seem filled with the intent
to be lost that their loss is no disaster.

Lose something every day. Accept the fluster
of lost door keys, the hour badly spent.
The art of losing isn't hard to master.

Then practice losing farther, losing faster:
places, and names, and where it was you meant
to travel. None of these will bring disaster.

I lost my mother's watch. And look! my last, or
next-to-last, of three loved houses went.
The art of losing isn't hard to master.

I lost two cities, lovely ones. And, vaster,
some realms I owned, two rivers, a continent.
I miss them, but it wasn't a disaster.

– Even losing you (the joking voice, a gesture
I love) I shan't have lied. It's evident
the art of losing's not too hard to master
though it may look like (*Write* it!) like disaster.

ADRIENNE RICH

Dialogue

She sits with one hand poised against her head, the
other turning an old ring to the light
for hours our talk has beaten
like rain against the screens
a sense of August and heat-lightning
I get up, go to make tea, come back
we look at each other
then she says (and this is what I live through
over and over) – she says: *I do not know*
if sex is an illusion

I do not know
who I was when I did those things
or who I said I was
or whether I willed to feel
what I had read about
or who in fact was there with me
or whether I knew, even then
that there was doubt about these things

1972

For a Russian Poet

1. The winter dream

Everywhere, snow is falling. Your bandaged foot
drags across huge cobblestones, bells
hammer in distant squares.
Everything we stood against has conquered
and now we're part
of it all. *Life's the main thing,* I hear you say,
but a fog is spreading between this landmass
and the one your voice
mapped so long for me. All that's visible
is walls, endlessly yellow-grey, where
so many risks were taken, the shredded skies
slowly littering both our continents with
the only justice left, burying
footprints, bells and voices with all deliberate speed.

1967

2. Summer in the country

Now, again, every year for years: the life-and-death talk,
late August, forebodings
under the birches, along the water's edge
and between the typed lines

and evenings, tracing a pattern of absurd hopes
in broken nutshells
                              but this year we both
sit after dark with the radio
unable to read, unable to write

trying the blurred edges of broadcasts
for a little truth, taking a walk before bed
wondering what a man can do, asking that
at the verge of tears in a lightning-flash of loneliness.

3. *The demonstration*

'Natalya Gorbanevskaya
13/3 Novopeschanaya Street
Apartment 34

At noon we sit down quietly on the parapet
and unfurl our banners
                        almost immediately
the sound of police whistles
from all corners of Red Square
                        we sit
quietly and offer no resistance – '

Is this your little boy – ?

we will relive this over and over

the banners torn
from our hands
            blood flowing
a great jagged torn place
in the silence of complicity

that much at least
we did here

In your flat, drinking tea
waiting for the police
your children asleep while you write
quickly, the letters you want to get off
before tomorrow

I'm a ghost at your table
touching poems in a script I can't read

we'll meet each other later

August 1968

Jerusalem

In my dream, children
are stoning other children
with blackened carob-pods
I dream my son is riding
on an old grey mare
to a half-dead war
on a dead-grey road
through the cactus and thistles
and dried brook-beds.

In my dream, children
are swaddled in smoke
and their uncut hair smolders
even here, here
where trees have no shade
and rocks have no shadow
trees have no memories
only the stones and
the hairs of the head.

I dream his hair is growing
and has never been shorn
from slender temples hanging
like curls of barbed wire
and his first beard is growing
smoldering like fire
his beard is smoke and fire
and I dream him riding
patiently to the war.

What I dream of the city
is how hard it is to leave
and how useless to walk
outside the blasted walls
picking up the shells
from a half-dead war
and I wake up in tears

and hear the sirens screaming
and the carob-tree is bare.

Balfour Street
July 1966

MARILYN HACKER

La Vie de Château
– a fiction

That morning, she crisply snapped a postcard
next to his cup. 'I think this is for you,'
she said. *Bugger! How does that girl
know where I am?* 'How does that girl know where
you are? Only my husband and the servants
know you've come here.' 'And the children.'

'Is she in correspondence with your *children?*'
'Hardly.' He smiled, rereading the postcard,
accepted through a swath of sun the servant's
proffered brioches, and more steamed milk. '*Are* you
going to explain?' Postcards fluttered from nowhere,
like the too-clever fingers of the girl.

It wouldn't do to think about the girl.
'I think that I'll go for a drive with the children
this morning.' 'I think that you'll go nowhere
until you explain.' It was almost a rude postcard.
Well, quite rude. How *did* she know? How could you
explain one to the other? Now the servants

had left. He couldn't accustom himself to servants,
or didn't like to think he could. The girl
who ironed, dark and thin, an arrogant smile you
wanted to decipher . . . His children and her children
shouted in the orchard. He'd sent *her* a postcard,
of course. She hadn't sniffed him out of nowhere

with a very naked man headed for nowhere
running like hell (the older woman servant
sailed the plates off) – a British Museum postcard
of a Greek vase. 'Let's forget that wretched girl.
I thought I'd have Françoise take all the children
swimming, and spend the morning alone with you.'

'Yes, lovely, I'd like to spend the morning with you.'
Blonde and blue air, a morning for getting nowhere.
Already he regretted the drive with the children,
regretted, really, consigning them to servants
on their holiday. Could they forget the girl
by lunch? He might send her another postcard.

'What are you looking at?' 'Nothing. White lace. The servant's
apron.' 'I know where we'll go.' Grappling the girl
like children in the dark. He'd send a postcard.

Villanelle: Late Summer

I love you and it makes me rather dull
when everyone is voluble and gay.
The conversation hits a certain lull.

I moon, rattled as china in a bull-
shop, wanting to go, wanting to stay.
I love you and it makes me rather dull.

You might think I had cotton in my skull.
And why is one in Staithes and not in Hay?
The conversation hits a certain lull.

You took a fretful, unoriginal
and unrelaxing friend on holiday.
I love you and it makes me rather dull.

A sheepish sky, with puffs of yellow wool,
watches the tide interrogate the bay.
The conversation hits a certain lull.

And I am grimly silent, swollen full
of unsaid things. I certainly can't say

'I love you.' And it makes me rather dull.
The conversation hits a certain lull.

The Last Time

Somebody has endlessly postponed
this summer; it is chilly and uncertain
as you, my own, not in the least my own.
I watched clouds move through the organza curtain
all afternoon. The noises of the farm
and loud birds ravaging Tom's kitchen garden
break on my book. Untrustworthy, the light
shifts every hour, wind sun fog sun wind storm.
I can't blame you, or ask your pardon,
or dream the day into another night

and wake up foundering between self-pity
and despair, the way I did today,
and take a morning train back to the city
where nothing much will happen anyway,
dubious individuals will write
dubious poetry, children will get cuffed
for nothing, and not forget it, I will fault
everyone fastidiously, tight-
assed and sceptical, obscure enough
to get away with it. O could I halt

this headfirst fall and rest love in your green
approval, tasting you like certainty,
summer would certainly start, something clean
and mobile as hill winds would move with me
and I would do . . . No, I do not believe
any of this, invoke it when I fear
the dull immobile speechless bland inert
mad lady who sits in me when I leave,
comfy as anything. Through her queer
nerveless hide, nothing pleasures, nothing hurts,

she could sit in the same place all day, all day,
not seeing, not hearing, not deaf, not blind,

her eyes like marbles and her flanks like whey;
the Sow reposes sated on my mind,
sated on what would have been a clean
if bitter lyric, setting me apart
from people who can say, 'I did,' 'I thought,'
as real things. I have said what I mean,
more than I meant; and if I start
over, from the beginning, if she bought

my silence with that other fear: you will
always be alone, I will console
you, I would have to be still
or tell lies, if I believed in a soul,
damn it, if I believed in my art, fake
it. And I will believe in that,
if necessary, as an act of will,
and she, stuporous lunatic, makes me make
poems; more than love or fame, her flat
face presses inside my face; she spills

through me, hypoglycaemic languor
paralyzing rage, her rage, my rage.
Poles: pain and insensibility, anger
and absence, the senile queen, the murdering page.
He keeps me up all night. She makes me sleep
all day. Now clogged and vague, I maul the pain
to shape. They'll never let me out. Or I'm
not going. Anyway, not off the deep
end. Lovely people, I won't come again.
This is the last time. (That was the last time.)

BARBARA GUEST

Circassians

I become excited when I am with Circassians
I am almost in despair.
        That cousin with his moustaches

they seem to know what to do
    with sadness and ecstasy
almost like the Irish

and who am I with my mixed feelings?

    I put down my pen
and I have found a pencil
    not any pencil
    but this one fabricated in Germany

I bought it in France.

Caroline has asked me to lunch.
We eat a steak
cucumbers
radishes
we drink vodka. Polish vodka.

    I look at photographs.
They are her grandparents in front of their tent.

    Grandfather
is dressed in his tunic and pants.
    His belt carries a knife.
His blouse and his blossoming pantaloon
    is the way I should describe them.
His wife is shy and she too billows.

    We are in a village
    at the top of the mountain
    look at that drop!

Those are her grandparents.

Caroline too is photographed.
On the beach at Amagansett
    look how it shows
    her face of the Caucasus
    even the sloped eyelids
    the tense skin near the eyes!

How remarkable she is!

Caroline is many versts
from Yahni Polyana

Caroline's apartment is
in New York City

We are neighbors and we admire each other.

Have some vodka.

Roses
'painting has no air . . .'
— GERTRUDE STEIN

That there should never be air
in a picture surprises me.
It would seem to be only a picture
of a certain kind, a portrait in paper
or glued, somewhere a stickiness
as opposed to a stick-to-it-ness
of another genre. It might be
quite new to do without
that air, or to find oxygen
on the landscape line
like a boat which is an object
or a shoe which never floats
and is stationary.

                    Still there
are certain illnesses that require
air, lots of it. And there are nervous
people who cannot manufacture
enough air and must seek
for it when they don't have plants,
in pictures. There is the mysterious
traveling that one does outside
the cube and this takes place
in air.

It is why one develops
an attitude toward roses picked
in the morning air, even roses
without sun shining on them.
The roses of Juan Gris from which
we learn the selflessness of roses
existing perpetually without air,
the lid being down, so to speak,
withal a 1912 fragrance sifting
to the left corner where we read
'La Merveille' and escape.

Even Ovid

The vivid report of your gracious diehardedness
has wounded me, expecting the palm leaf
in a forwarded letter, not realizing
the dismal street was our way of greeting.
Special azure was once our way
and we beneath umbrellas nodded,
so tenderly we born on the cusp and knowing
it when suns struck and the moons
at your fingertips were yellow as that cloud
over the rooftop which today is a pompier
and the burning trees will assemble themselves.
I too am minute as ashes with the fine
grain of my feeling running crisscross into dark
where I sight you enviously at the blurred roots
and the ospreys play there, they have second sight
like sponges, loving both canal and river,
commuting as you on water, fearful of this group
of buildings, even going underground.
You like it because your eyes see further,
even as a rock quarry is graceful
with your initials at the sorrowful poem's end.

The Interruptions

It is a landscape inhabited by Baudelaire
  his *îles*, his *fantômes*, his *sang*
the faithful birds with their quick orgasm
the agility of the wave that attacks and plunders
  bruised bones, pallor and sleeplessness,
the fresh sand the treading skies and Spring
  a murderess in her photographer's gown

Rather it was the way I felt that morning, having
dreamed of a person who drew my blood there
in the shadow of the pier a frantic projection
having been permitted to exclude all care
and taste from its beams
there like a shingled and iron albatross
it lay with faint breathing on the sand
that was on its way to becoming prepared
to be a much larger station; that is the truth
of what lay before us and what we lay on
making telephone calls with air running
over the legs and into the palms which held
the voices with their visions of days this version
partitioned by explanations of why
the letter L had so much strength due to the extra
line attached to the vertical certain persons
becoming famous and even happy after this discovery
then dying overnight.

This tells you why my impartial sadness
needs you and desires you in this part of the Covenant
because you are a native especially through your shoulders
where all the wild chasms and snow boundaries
have been captivated and subdued
changed from missionaries into ravens
the fanciful hippity hopping being
your way of breaking into me through the pantry's door
on your path to the bible and the snug windows
the storm a little over to the left where the wince

is clouding in on you and on your eyes
of a natural brown like a barn or a spout
where the nest of eggs waits to determine its
eventual size after the gusts and the rain

Your fear of nature – no laughing matter –
like mine and Poe's
if you notice Baudelaire stayed close to the city
although Paris and her environs give us notice of few
lapses in taste where planning is concerned
those acres being confined to plots
and sacred wildernesses where
one can escape to the country at a minute's
notice and read Childe Harold surrounded
by verbena under oaks in a familiar arrondissement
yet that might make you nervous
remind you of home and its haunts –

An apprehension, not stepping in puddles,
and gluing your eyes to the spot beyond the horizon
a fixed stare of multiples and hues yet desperate
all the same like a bird in its covert
or an acorn on a bush or the quatrain soughing
the grass at sunset where we stood
after the toast and the kiss lifting what was lust
to the instant's light before its retreat
into dusk where the evil papers glow

LOUISE GLÜCK

Gratitude

Do not think I am not grateful for your small
kindness to me.
I like small kindnesses.
In fact I actually prefer them to the more
substantial kindness, that is always eyeing you,
like a large animal on a rug,

until your whole life reduces
to nothing but waking up morning after morning
cramped, and the bright sun shining on its tusks.

Flowering Plum

In spring from the black branches of the flowering plum tree
the woodthrush issues its routine
message of survival. Where does such happiness come from
as the neighbors' daughter reads into that singing,
and matches? All afternoon she sits
in the partial shade of the plum tree, as the mild wind
floods her immaculate lap with blossoms, greenish white
and white, leaving no mark, unlike
the fruit that will inscribe
unraveling dark stains in heavier winds, in summer.

CELIA GILBERT

Clyde

Clyde, you were older
than the other fourth graders;
your chalky face set off
with slick, black hair,
your lips too red.
When you smiled your mouth
went thick as a slug,
and when I turned my head in class
you were always there
like a dream I couldn't wake from,
bent over your work,
those pictures you drew and made us
look at: naked women and on *those* places
dark scribbles.

Clyde, you said
you'd get me after school and

kiss me, and I hid in the girls' room
until the janitor made me leave.
There you were behind the hedge.
I ran and ran, heart pounding,
looking over my shoulder.

You didn't even care about grownups.
You sneered at Miss Pyle's freckled hands,
called her a pillow tied in the middle.

Clyde, what about the morning
the bell rang and when we went in
someone whispered you were dead.
You hanged yourself. In the closet.

In my mind, I saw you swinging
in a crack of light through the half-shut door.
They said your mother told you
you were bad, you wouldn't stop
she was going to send you away
again.
Then, Clyde, you who sat in Miss Pyle's class,
one of us,
you went to your room.
Your wet laugh stopped.
You left me to the dark.

The Silence

The child is called from the garden,
away from the pond where the daylilies grow
and a frog punctuates the long hours.

'What's in your hand?' the uncle wants to know,
his voice and the others, always intruding.
She shakes them off if she can, but now,

caught, sullen and excited, she comes
leaving, in the grass, in the trees,
her armies waiting. Across her palm,

a newt stretches its lifeline, brown palpitation
flecked with orange suns. On her moist skin
she feels his appeal for her protection.

'Do you know what it is?' the grandmother demands.
She glowers, dumb with contempt and exaltation.
Let them have the last word.

The light records her ragged braids,
one blue rubber band, one red,
and over her heart, the shadow of a breast.

BEATRICE HAWLEY

Stones

These stones have not been arranged.
In the country of monuments along every path,
this is the border along the coast,
these are the leavings from the mountain of angels.
The dolphins who copy the angels are sleeping
they do not see me bruise my feet.

When I come here there is no moon.
The stones must be ordered by remembering
light cast by dancers. I cannot find the stone
with only the memory of a streetlamp miles away.
I use my hands to test the weight of each,
I move down closer. I touch them with my tongue.

They taste salt. I believe in mineral properties.
When I find the right monument I will taste it.
I will swallow it, I will carry it in my belly.
I will never drown. The marble will not sink.
I will be buried near water. My hair will grow
when I die, a tree will bloom from my eyes.

The one will be right that holds the light
from the body of a young swimmer who drowned.
The stone will seem at home among the others,

these others that pretend to be children
playing at the water's edge. They are liars.
They are old men who fell out of little boats.

They are old fishermen who never swam:
they hate the sea. The sea is a machine
with long chains to pull them in.
The sea is a machine which rubs them together;
they are polished, gleaming, they are like babies –
if I could see, they would trick me.

Every night I come here and put new stones in my mouth.
Every night the new stones fail me.
In the morning I am never invisible.
I always have to go back along the road,
the fishermen greet me on their way
to the small boats, their eyes are full of light.

The Wife's Poem

The animals are asleep,
the children are covered,
the mother is standing in the hall
leaning her arms into the sky.
She can't sleep. She watches
the dark spaces crack with light.

The husband is moaning.
He is having a nightmare about lions.
Her hand is there, soothing
him over to a dream of water.
She knows this will not last:
she will break or learn to sleep.

Her hand in the future will be settling
small things down in their corners,
folding a narrow blanket,
hemming thin curtains
for the room with one window only
she will live in alone.

AMY CLAMPITT

Stacking the Straw

In those days the oatfields'
fenced-in vats of running platinum,
the yellower alloy of wheat and barley,
whose end, however gorgeous all that trammeled
rippling in the wind, came down
to toaster-fodder, cereal
as a commodity, were a rebuke
to permanence – to bronze or any metal
less utilitarian than the barbed braids
that marked off a farmer's property,
or the stoked dinosaur of a steam engine
that made its rounds from farm to farm,
after the grain was cut and bundled,
and powered the machine that did the threshing.

Strawstacks' beveled loaves, a shape
that's now extinct, in those days were
the nearest thing the region had
to monumental sculpture. While hayracks
and wagons came and went, delivering bundles,
carting the winnowed ore off to the granary,

a lone man with a pitchfork stood aloft
beside the hot mouth of the blower,
building about himself, forkful
by delicately maneuvered forkful,
a kind of mountain, the golden
stuff of mulch, bedding for animals.
I always thought of him with awe –

a craftsman whose evolving altitude
gave him the aura of a hero. He'd come down
from the summit of the season's effort
black with the baser residues of that
discarded gold. Saint Thomas of Aquino
also came down from the summit

of a lifetime's effort, and declared
that everything he'd ever done was straw.

Tepoztlán

The Aztecs, conquering, brought Huitzilopochtli
and ceremonial slitting the heart out; Cortés,
a.k.a. Son of the Sun, along with new weapons,
El Señor and the Virgin of the Remedies,
introduced heaven and hell (which the Tepoztecans
never quite took hold of); the gringos
arrived with sanitary arrangements
and a great many questions.
                              Autonomy
climbed down from the plane empty-handed,
carrying only introspection and a few
self-canceling tropisms, innocent
of history as any peasant, to travel,
all in a day, from upland maguey fields'
clumped pewter prongs through treetop regions
where songbirds bright as parrots flashed
uncaged, living free as fishes; alongside
churches of ice-cream-tinted stone
carved like a barbed music, and vendors
of a poisoned rainbow – *helados, refrescos,*
nopals, papayas, mangos, melons all swarming
with warned-against amoebas – down
through villages smelling of pulque,
jasmine and dysentery; past haciendas
torpid with dust, the dogs owned by nobody,
the burros, whether led or tethered, all
long-suffering rancor, the stacked coffins
waiting, mainly child-size (fatality,
part jaguar, part hummingbird, part
gila monster, alive and well here,
clearly needs children); through the daily
dust-laying late-afternoon rainstorm,
in cadenced indigenous place-names

the drip of a slow waterfall,
or of foliage when the rain stops –
arriving, just after sundown,
at the town of Tepoztlán.
                                     Autonomy,
unaware that in some quarters
the place was famous, saw hanging
cliffs dyed a terrible heart-color
in the gloaming light; a marketplace
empty of people; a big double-towered
church whose doors stood open. No one
inside but a sexton in white *calzoni*,
sweeping up a litter that appeared
to be mainly jasmine: so much fragrance,
so much death, such miracles – El Señor,
glitter-skirted, casketed upright in glass –
such silence . . . until, for no known reason,
overhead the towered bells broke out
into such a pounding that bats, shaken
from their hooked-accordion sleep
by the tumult, poured onto the dark,
a river of scorched harbingers
from an underworld the Tepoztecans
don't altogether believe in.
                                     They speak
on occasion of Los Aires, or, in their
musical Nahuatl, of *Huehuetzintzin*,
the Old Ones. Who knows what ultimately
is, and what's mere invention? Autonomy,
encapsuled and enmembraned hitherto
by a deaf anxiety, left Tepoztlán
marked, for the first time ever,
by the totally unlooked-for – by a
halfway belief that from out there,
astoundingly, there might be,
now and then, some message.

Salvage

Daily the cortege of crumpled
defunct cars
goes by by the lasagna-
layered flatbed
truckload: hardtop

reverting to tar smudge,
wax shine antiqued to crusted
winepress smear,
windshield battered to
intact ice-tint, a rarity

fresh from the Pleistocene.
I like it; privately
I find aesthetic
satisfaction in these
ceremonial removals

from the category of
received ideas
to regions where pigeons'
svelte smoke-velvet
limousines, taxiing

in whirligigs, reclaim
a parking lot,
and the bag-laden
hermit woman, disencumbered
of a greater incubus,

the crush of unexamined
attitudes, stoutly
follows her routine,
mining the mountainsides
of our daily refuse

for artifacts: subversive
re-establishing
with each arcane

trash-basket dig
the pleasures of the ruined.

CAROLYN FORCHÉ

The Memory of Elena

We spend our morning
in the flower stalls counting
the dark tongues of bells
that hang from ropes waiting
for the silence of an hour.
We find a table, ask for *paella*,
cold soup and wine, where a calm
light trembles years behind us.

In Buenos Aires only three
years ago, it was the last time his hand
slipped into her dress, with pearls
cooling her throat and bells like
these, chipping at the night –

As she talks, the hollow
clopping of a horse, the sound
of bones touched together.
The *paella* comes, a bed of rice
and *camarones*, fingers and shells,
the lips of those whose lips
have been removed, mussels
the soft blue of a leg socket.

This is not *paella*, this is what
has become of those who remained
in Buenos Aires. This is the ring
of a rifle report on the stones,
her hand over her mouth,
her husband falling against her.

These are the flowers we bought
this morning, the dahlias tossed
on his grave and bells
waiting with their tongues cut out
for this particular silence.
1977

The Visitor

In Spanish he whispers there is no time left.
It is the sound of scythes arcing in wheat,
the ache of some field song in Salvador.
The wind along the prison, cautious
as Francisco's hands on the inside, touching
the walls as he walks, it is his wife's breath
slipping into his cell each night while he
imagines his hand to be hers. It is a small country.

There is nothing one man will not do to another.
1979

Departure

We take it with us, the cry
of a train slicing a field
leaving its stiff suture, a distant
tenderness as when rails slip
behind us and our windows
touch the field, where it seems
the dead are awake and so reach
for each other. Your hand
cups the light of a match
to your mouth, to mine, and I want
to ask if the dead hold
their mouths in their hands like this
to know what is left of them.
Between us, a tissue of smoke,
a bundle of belongings, luggage
that will seem to float beside us,

the currency we will change
and change again. Here is the name
of a friend who will take you in,
the papers of a man who vanished,
the one you will become when
the man you have been disappears.
I am the woman whose photograph
you will not recognize, whose face
emptied your eyes, whose eyes
were brief, like the smallest
of cities we slipped through.

The Colonel

What you have heard is true. I was in his house. His wife carried a
tray of coffee and sugar. His daughter filed her nails, his son went out
for the night. There were daily papers, pet dogs, a pistol on the
cushion beside him. The moon swung bare on its black cord over the
house. On the television was a cop show. It was in English. Broken
bottles were embedded in the walls around the house to scoop the
kneecaps from a man's legs or cut his hands to lace. On the windows
there were gratings like those in liquor stores. We had dinner, rack of
lamb, good wine, a gold bell was on the table for calling the maid.
The maid brought green mangoes, salt, a type of bread. I was asked
how I enjoyed the country. There was a brief commercial in Spanish.
His wife took everything away. There was some talk then of how
difficult it had become to govern. The parrot said hello on the
terrace. The colonel told it to shut up, and pushed himself from the
table. My friend said to me with his eyes: say nothing. The colonel
returned with a sack used to bring groceries home. He spilled many
human ears on the table. They were like dried peach halves. There is
no other way to say this. He took one of them in his hands, shook it in
our faces, dropped it into a water glass. It came alive there. I am tired
of fooling around he said. As for the rights of anyone, tell your
people they can go fuck themselves. He swept the ears to the floor
with his arm and held the last of his wine in the air. Something for
your poetry, no? he said. Some of the ears on the floor caught this

scrap of his voice. Some of the ears on the floor were pressed to the
ground.
May 1978

CLARIBEL ALEGRÍA

Everything is Normal in our Backyard

And in spite of the sun
the air
the doves
the inquisitor goes on
tending his roses
removes weeds
stones
gnarled roots
he turns the earth
looks again
keeps off
the marchioness
as always at her crochet-work
every time someone goes by
her glasses fall off
slight shifts in tone
to indicate rank
the lonely man dances
longing to smash his shadow
into a thousand pieces
the one they crucified
is getting old
no-one listens any more
to his prophecies
the iconoclastic
clown goes over to him
and places in his mouth
a cigarette
have a drag boss

have a drag
but he spits it out
and the squatting beggar
picks it up
the clouds shimmer
a fragrance of jasmine rises
along the walls
the jailer
walks by dressed in white
looks for his friend
the priest
the hangman has arrived
and it is time
check
declares the general
his partner starts
with fright
he blocks it with his bishop
mate
the general fires
and the victim
topples headlong
I leave the inquisitor
crushing insects
everything is normal
in our backyard
with fists
feet saliva
two guys are fighting
one wants
the other to tell him
he knows that he knows
he does not know
nor does the other
the psychiatrist leans over
I try hard not to say
Old man God
which of them is right?

I do say it
I make a point of it
I wait
he smiles
and asks:
How are your verses
coming along?

The American Way of Death

If you scrabble the mountain day and night
and lie in ambush behind the shrubs
(the pack-failure is growing,
thirst opens cracks in the throat
and the fever for change
devours you)
if you choose the *guerrilla*,
be careful,
they kill you.
If you combat your chaos
through peace,
non-violence,
brotherly love,
the long marches without guns
with women and children
being spat at in the face,
be careful,
they kill you.

If your skin is dark
and you go bare-foot
and your insides are gnawed by worms,
hunger,
malaria:
slowly they kill you.

If you are a negro from Harlem
and they offer you football pitches
paved with asphalt

a television in the kitchen
and leaves of marijuana:
bit by bit they kill you.

If you suffer from asthma
if a dream exasperates you
– whether in Buenos Aires
or Atlanta –
that takes you from Montgomery
to Memphis

or across the mountains on foot,
be careful:
you will become obsessed
a sleepwalker
a poet.

If you are born in the ghetto
or shanty town
and your school is the gutter
or the street corner,
first of all you must eat,
then pay the rent
and in time left over
sit on the pavement
and watch the cars go by.

But one day the news reaches you,
by word of mouth
your neighbour tells you
because you can't read
or don't have five cents
to buy the newspaper
or the television has packed up:
whichever way,
you learn the news:
they have killed him,
yes,
they have killed someone of yours.

KATHLEEN JAMIE

Black Spiders

He looked up to the convent
she'd gone to. She answered no questions
but he knew by the way she'd turned away
that morning.
He felt like swimming to the caves.

*

The nuns have retreated. The eldest still
peals the bell in glee, although no-one comes
from the ruins. All their praying was done
when they first saw the ships and the Turks'
swords reflecting the sun.

In the convent the cistern is dry,
the collection boxes empty – cleft skulls
severed and bleached,
are kept in a shrine, and stare to the East.

*

She caught sight of him later, below, brushing salt
from the hair of his nipples. She wanted them
to tickle; black spiders on her lips.

Storm in Istanbul

Beware the temper of the only god.
We asked only rain to smother the dust.

By three we'd kicked off the single grey sheet.
The patrol passed in the alley.

We took it for a torch, a search, we could not speak
above the roar, we opened a window
and heard the boots. Leaned out, tongues out
to taste the rain.

In the flash you could read the armoured car's plate
The guard saw moving shapes, fired
shouts between the cracking of petrified cloud.
He laughed too loud when
he linked arms with his chum
('Thought you was a terrorist, didn'I?')
Their uniforms scraped.

You could have shot him from here,
some mother's gaunt son. Not even having
his big boots on could save him
from flinching when his almighty blue mosque
was lit from above.
He crouched below his bayonet. It gleamed
like the minarets jabbing the sky
that shuddered and roared in pain.

Beside the rancid heap where it eats a dog wept.
All the cats howled. It gave him
the creeps. He whispered through his teeth
to calm them. For him
someone began to play a pipe,
a few shaking voices sang. Light was coming . . .

From the towers came the wail of a failing old imam.

The faithful went to pray.
The heathen, we slept.

VALERIE GILLIES

Bomber

You too must live; and must know how
in the wicked city, everyone sleeps
alongside you, bomber, as they show
by the twitch in their dream when you meet.

You with your smoking briefcase
and the warm gun hidden in your breast,

with that young and Irish-looking face
you get trapped in the tube like a small firecrest.

And nothing is so much like the head
imprinted on the holy shroud to this day,
as your head; thorns are in the blood you shed,
roping thickly down your brow in the subway.

Inaccurate as your short chemical fuse
you flared too soon, flung the five-pounder
down the carriage and broke loose
to run up the sidings, already hounded.

Among the shards of hurtling metal
you shot and killed a man, a black:
then turned the gun upon yourself,
crying, You English bastards! at your back.

With Gaelic poverty, you are half-alive:
a police artist drew your picture from the hospital
as handsome but evil, obsessed to die.
He sent it out as the image of a criminal.

Housed in the same building as your victims,
they have you: detectives ring your bedside.
They found your old landlord, too, to tell your sin:
He said you were clean, quiet, considerate, blue-eyed.

Now London's limbs associate with each other,
feeling to find if an arm is lost, a leg is kept.
But, man with all the dead brothers,
what corpse are you trying to lay on our doorstep?

Harrowing

From the whitewashed farmhouse in the tilted glen
she is looking out and watching him connect
horse-traces to harrows, grass-grown in the yard.
His collie with the broken teeth hangs back
by the gin-trap glint of the harrow tines.

He is putting the draught horse in harness;
all of seventeen hands it is, but it won't pull
into the feel of cold strap and bar against its breast.
She runs to the sheds for a rag to wrap around.
When she comes back they are beating it.

Three of them are taking it in turn, putting out
their strength to raise great weals along its back.
Tree-bark gashed, it makes no sound.
Not dumb, she cries 'Let me at you, I'll kill you!'
It takes two to drag her off and lock her in.

Rage raises her red face against the window.
'Walk on!' The wounds are on earth's back
where Duncan goes stumbling over clods,
peering round harrowed flanks to see the line
of his work, going to pulverize the soil.

LIZ LOCHHEAD

Poppies

My father said she'd be fined
at best, jailed maybe, the lady
whose high heels shattered the silence.
I sat on his knee, we were listening
to the silence on the radio.
My mother tutted, oh that it was terrible,
as over our air
those sharp heeltaps struck steel, rang clear
as a burst of gunfire or a laugh
through those wired-up silent streets around the Cenotaph.
Respect.
Remembrance.
Surely when all was said
three minutes silence in November
wasn't much to ask for, for the dead?
Poppies on the mantelpiece, the photograph

of a boy in a forage cap, the polished
walnut veneer of the wireless,
the buzzing in the ears and when
the silence ended the heldfire voice
of the commentator, who was shocked,
naturally, but not
wanting to make too much of it.
Why did she do it?
Was she taken sick – but that was no
excuse, on the radio it said,
couldn't you picture it?
how grown soldiers buttoned in their uniforms
keeled over, fell like flies
trying to keep up the silence.
Maybe it was looking at the khaki button eye
and the woundwire stem
of the redrag poppy
pinned in her proper lapel
that made the lady stick a bloody bunch of them
behind her ear
and clash those high heels across the square,
a dancer.

My Rival's House

is peopled with many surfaces.
Ormolu and gilt, slipper satin,
lush velvet couches,
cushions so stiff you can't sink in.
Tables polished clear enough to see distortions in.

We take our shoes off at her door,
shuffle stocking-soled, tiptoe – the parquet floor
is beautiful and its surface must
be protected. Dust
cover, drawn shade,
won't let the surface colour fade.

Silver sugar-tongs and silver salver
my rival serves us tea.
She glosses over him and me.
I am all edges, a surface, a shell
and yet my rival thinks she means me well.
But what squirms beneath her surface I can tell.
Soon, my rival
capped tooth, polished nail
will fight, fight foul for her survival.
Deferential, daughterly, I sip
and thank her nicely for each bitter cup.

And I have much to thank her for.
This son she bore –
first blood to her –
never, never can escape scot free
the sour potluck of family.
And oh how close
this family that furnishes my rival's place.

Lady of the house.
Queen bee.
She is far more unconscious
far more dangerous than me.
Listen, I was always my own worst enemy.
She has taken even this from me.

She dishes up her dreams for breakfast.
Dinner, and her salt tears pepper our soup.
She won't
give up.

ÁGNES GERGELY

Crazed Man in Concentration Camp
Tr. Edwin Morgan

All through the march, besides bag and blanket
he carried in his hands two packages of empty boxes,

and when the company halted for a couple of minutes
he laid the two packages of empty boxes neatly at each side,
being careful not to damage or break either of them,
the parcels were of
ornamental boxes
dovetailed by sizes each to each
and tied together with packing-cord,
the top box with a picture on it.
When the truck was about to start, the sergeant
shouted something in sergeant's language,
they sprang up suddenly,
and one of the boxes rolled down to the wheel,
the smallest one, the one with the picture:
'It's fallen,' he said and made to go after it,
but the truck moved off
and his companions held his hands
while his hands held the two packages of boxes
and his tears trailed down his jacket.
'It's fallen,' he said that evening in the queue –
and it meant nothing to him to be shot dead.

Sign on My Door Jamb
Tr. Thomas Land

In memoriam my father

I do not cherish memories
and those I have I do not safeguard.
I do not seek forgotten graveyards.
Bio-chemistry doesn't move me.

Yet at times like this towards November
as fog-damped windows seal my room
and I gasp for air and long for relief,
I sense your invisible rise
as from the waters of the mind
and odd gestures of yours re-emerge.

I sense your long and nervous fingers
arranging a thermos flask and pocket knife

with the Bible and warm underclothes
and an old can opener in the gaping
green knapsack; and under the weightless load
you can carry, I sense your back's surprise.

I sense your departure, elegant tramp, from the house:
you'd never go away, you just set out,
and look back laughing, aged thirty-eight years,
and you nod and you gesture, *I'll soon return*
(tomorrow would have been your birthday)
while your tears dribble inwards whining
and you wave – and how you wave!

Sign on my door jamb, you've remained;
the bars, the bridge, the sludgy road,
the gorging of grass, the fatal empty weakness
are only freak inventions of the mind;
for I have lied, I often see you
beneath the stifling, low November sky;
you set out with me, you breathe, and your tears
I let your tears go dribbling down my throat;
and where it had fallen, the thin
cigarette struck from your mouth
has burned on a star ever since.

MARGARET ATWOOD

The Reincarnation of Captain Cook

Earlier than I could learn
the maps had been coloured in.
When I pleaded, the kings told me
nothing was left to explore.

I set out anyway, but
everywhere I went
there were historians, wearing
wreaths and fake teeth
belts; or in the deserts, cairns

and tourists. Even the caves had
candle stubs, inscriptions quickly
scribbled in darkness. I could

never arrive. Always
the names got there before.

Now I am old I know my
mistake was my acknowledging
of maps. The eyes raise
tired monuments.

Burn down
the atlases, I shout
to the park benches; and go

past the cenotaph
waving a blank banner
across the street, beyond
the corner

into a new land cleaned of geographies,
its beach gleaming with arrows.

The Shadow Voice

My shadow said to me:
What is the matter

Isn't the moon warm
enough for you
Why do you need
the blanket of another body

Whose kiss is moss

Around the picnic tables
the bright pink hands hold sandwiches
crumbled by distance. Flies crawl
over the sweet instant

You know what is in those baskets

The trees outside are bending with
children shooting guns. Leave
them alone. They are playing
games of their own.

I give water, I give clean crusts

Aren't there enough words
flowing in your veins
to keep you going

The Surveyors

By the felled trees, their stems
snipped neatly as though by scissors
we could tell where they had been,
the surveyors,
        clearing
their trail of single reason
(with a chainsaw it was easy
as ruling a line with a pencil)
through a land where geometries are multiple.

We followed the cut stumps,
their thumbprints, measurements
blazed in red paint: numbers and brash
letters, incongruous against
sheared wood or glacial rock

and we saw too how these vivid
signals, painted assertions

were as we looked surrounded, changed
by the gradual pressures of endless
green on the eyes, the diffused
weight of summer, the many branches

to signs without motion, red arrows
pointing in no directions; faint ritual
markings leached by time
of any meaning:

red vestiges of an erased
people, a broken
line

At The Tourist Centre in Boston

There is my country under glass,
a white relief-
map with red dots for the cities,
reduced to the size of a wall

and beside it ten blownup snapshots
one for each province,
in purple-browns and odd reds,
the green of the trees dulled;
all blues however
of an assertive purity.

Mountains and lakes and more lakes
(though Quebec is a restaurant and Ontario the empty
interior of the parliament buildings),
with nobody climbing the trails and hauling out
the fish and splashing in the water

but arrangements of grinning tourists –
look here, Saskatchewan
is a flat lake, some convenient rocks
where two children pose with a father
and the mother is cooking something
in immaculate slacks by a smokeless fire,
her teeth white as detergent.

Whose dream is this, I would like to know;
is this a manufactured
hallucination, a cynical fiction, a lure
for export only?

I seem to remember people,
at least in the cities, also slush,
machines and assorted garbage. Perhaps
that was my private mirage

which will just evaporate
when I go back. Or the citizens will be gone,
run off to the peculiarly
green forests
to wait among the brownish mountains
for the platoons of tourists
and plan their odd red massacres.

Unsuspecting
window lady, I ask you:

Do you see nothing
watching you from under the water?

Was the sky ever that blue?

Who really lives there?

MIRIAM WADDINGTON

What is a Canadian

What is a Canadian
anyway? A mountain, a maple
leaf, a prairie, a Niagara fall,
a trail beside the Atlantic, a
bilingualism, a scarred mosaic,
a yes-no somehow-or-other maybe-
might-be should-be could-be
glacial shield, grain elevator,
empire daughter imperial order of
man woman child or what?

Beau-Belle

I'm in love with a clerk
from Trois Rivières
who trills his r's
and slicks his hair;

He's smooth as a seal
his smile is jolly,
though my name is Miriam
he calls me Polly;

He sends me greetings
on golden cards
and mails me snapshots
of snowy yards;

I'm *mauvaise anglaise* –
this he forgives,
between us two
it's live-and-let-lives;

He's in his city,
I'm in mine,
we meet at Easter
on Bleury and Pine;

He calls me Polly,
I call him Patrice,
he says *Madame
a votre service;*

And I say *Monsieur
dis-moi tu,
tu es poupé*
and I love you.

Back at York University

I'm back
and the profile of
Jackson Pollock stares
at me from a catalogue
cover in the jumble
on my desk; he makes
me want to cry over
the disorder of
everything human.

On the campus I pass
strange and terrible
Englishmen; albino eyes
dry umbrellas, giant
shadows and on the
bland blind faces of
Americans I read my fate:
the politics of exile
in my own country.

Where are we all
heading for who disappear
into Central Square into
coffee-shop into book-
store who are swallowed
into bullet elevators,
shot out into classrooms,
who rifle history push
our way into the past?

I am walking back
to an English colony,
watch me change into
an American aspiration,
look, I'm whispering into
a Canadian answer-box,
and not even the profile
of Jackson Pollock, his
suffering or my own
anger can stop it, so
it's high time for me to be
feeling this low.

Popular Geography

Miami is one big yellow
pantsuit where the ocean
is louder than the sighs
of old age; Chicago is

a huge hot gun sending
smoke into the sky for
1000 miles to Winnipeg;
New York is a bright sharp
hypodermic needle and the
Metropolitan Opera singing
Wagner on winter afternoons,
and my own Toronto is an
Eaton's charge account adding
to the music in a Henry Moore
skating rink; Montreal was
once an Iroquois city huddled
around a mountain under a cross
and now is the autoroute to
an Olympic dream; everything
has changed, all the cities
are different, but Manitoba
oh Manitoba, you are still
a beautiful green grain
elevator storing the sunlight
and growing out of the black
summer earth.

JENNY MASTORÁKI

Tr. Nikos Germanakos

The Vandals

Now they're pillaging the last coast.
In the activities of the Vandals
there was always a certain faith
that history would ultimately justify
the Dorians

Prometheus

Nights bring you the fever
of a Roman triumph.

The legionnaire, the goddess, the demagogue –
a slave whispers your name in his ear –
the hetaera with the redskin cheeks,
the bath attendant.
Just before the ceiling opens
and they all die, smothered in flowers,
you, having discovered fire,
hastily trade your liver.

The Death of a Warrior
Tr: Kimon Friar

The death of a warrior
should be slow and studied
like the distilled
transport of an adolescent
who becomes a man when he first makes love.
On his tomb place
two large question marks
for life and for death
and a traffic sign
that forbids
the passing of parades.

DAHLIA RAVIKOVITCH

Tr. Chana Block

The Horns of Hittin

The Horns of Hittin: site of a celebrated battle in which Saladin
decisively defeated the Crusader armies in 1187.

In the morning strange ships appeared on the sea,
prow and stern
in the ancient fashion.
In eleven hundred, bands of crusaders set sail,
kings and rabble.

Crates of gold and plunder piled up in the ports,
ships of gold
piers of gold.
The sun lit marvelous flames in them,
burning forests.
When the sun dazzled and the waves rocked,
they longed for Byzantium.
How cruel and simple the crusaders were.
They plundered everything.

Terror seized the villagers.
Those strangers carried off their daughters,
sired them blue-eyed grandsons
in shame,
shrugged off their honor.

Slender-necked ships set sail for Egypt.
The splendid troops struck at Acre,
a lightning force.
All of them swift knights bearing the Bishop's blessing.
A great flock of wolves.

How their eyes shone
when they saw the palm trees sway in the wind.
How they soiled their beards with spittle
when they dragged women into the brush.
They built many citadels,
snipers' towers and ramparts of basalt.
Their bastards in the villages
marvelled at them.

In twelve hundred, the Marquis of Montfort
grew faint.
The winds of Galilee whistled over his gloomy fortress.
A curved dagger burst from the East –
a jester's staff.
Saladin, in motley, advanced from the East.
With a ram's horns that infidel
gored them hip upon thigh,

punished them
at the Horns of Hittin.

No kingdom remained to them,
no life eternal,
no Jerusalem.
How cruel and simple the crusaders were.
They plundered everything.

Deep Calleth unto Deep

In Jerusalem I had my days of roses.
What is Jerusalem if not a hive of white houses?
I came there young and returned, years later,
like a stray thing.
Alone, in somebody's house,
I lifted my eyes to the hills
to see if help would come.

Clouds hunted one another,
dark pines breathed beneath me,
suddenly there fell from the ends of the West
a strange
splinter of the sun.

And my longings drenched me

and sawed in my head like a cricket
and swarmed like wasps inside me
I was that lost.

RIVKA MIRIAM

Tr. Linda Zisquit

The Stripes in Joseph's Coat

The stripes in Joseph's coat
like the rungs in the ladder of Jacob's dream.
The cloak was warm from the sun moon and stars

Sheaves flew off from it as Joseph walked.
In the pit as in the arms of his mother Rachel of the Well –
above Ishmaelites roamed about, their bells ringing
and on the humps of their camels they moved him
as in the heart of seas.
The camel rolls up its neck like a long arm
and bracelets leap in Joseph's eyes.
His mother hid the idols under her on the camel
pressing them to her like large dolls.
He touched them with a small finger
and they stabbed him with a larger finger
shooting him to Egypt.
The God of the Hebrews slept under him the whole way
like a large stone lumped together from many stones.

Miriam's Well

Miriam's well rolled in the desert
made of the mouths of fish.
The nation drinking from it
turned to water
and rolled after her in the desert
and the desert rolled after them like a carpet.
Rise up, well, sang the people
and their voices were a density of cloud
and the dryness quenched their voices.

Die in Me

Die in me.
Who by fire and who by water and who in the great abyss.
I extended a rose to you.
I stopped breathing.
Die in me die in me die in me
and darkness over the surface of the deep.

The Girl Who Drowned in the Well

The girl who drowned in the well
and they raised her from there, soft and dripping
and she left her face in the well
to go with it.
The girl whose dresses would rustle
left her face in the well. The whiteness of her face in the well.
Lord, she was thirsty.

EUNICE DE SOUZA

Marriages Are Made

My cousin Elena
is to be married.
The formalities
have been completed:
her family history examined
for T.B. and madness
her father declared solvent
her eyes examined for squints
her teeth for cavities
her stools for the possible
non-Brahmin worm.
She's not quite tall enough
and not quite full enough
(children will take care of that)
Her complexion it was decided
would compensate, being just about
the right shade
of rightness
to do justice to
Francisco X. Noronha Prabhu
good son of Mother Church.

He Speaks

Well, now tell me
what would you do to a
woman who wrote to you
saying: You haven't written
for three weeks. You're the
meanest man alive. Not even
an exclamation mark at the end
and she sends telegrams and
express letters saying it was
a joke, love, it was a joke.
I did what any self-respecting
man would. I ignored her for
a week. Her pleadings wore
me down. She was an affectionate
creature and tried hard, poor dear,
but never quite made the grade.
She *would* walk too close to me
and then protest naively: How
should lovers walk? Show me:
Ridiculous, too, her unseemly
mirth when I said confidentially:
I have such an hypnotic effect
on women. Everywhere I go
they fall into my arms.
Jamie Bond! she cried
My man in India's answer to
Jamie Bond!
After that pathological display
I decided there was only one
thing to do: fix her.
The next time we were making love
I said quite casually:
I hope you realize I do this
with other women.

Autobiographical

Right now, here it comes.
I killed my father when I was three.
I have muddled through several affairs
and always come out badly.
I've learned almost nothing from experience.
I head for the abyss with
monotonous regularity.

My enemies say I'm a critic because
really I'm writhing with envy
and anyway need to get married.

My friends say I'm not
entirely without talent.

Yes, I've tried suicide,
I tidied my clothes but
left no notes. I was surprised
to wake up in the morning.

One day my soul
stood outside me
watching me twitch
and grin and gibber
the skin tight
over my bones

I thought the whole world
was trying to rip me up
cut me down go through me
with a razor blade

then I discovered
a cliché: that's what I wanted
to do to the world.

SARAH KIRSCH

Before the Sun Rises
Tr. *Michael Hamburger*

Before the sun rises my brothers call the spotted dogs in the yard
blow their hands shake dew from their shoes before the sun is up my
brothers are behind the village have laid nets in the undergrowth
bind a bird up tightly it is blinded it sings right to the end the brothers
fill their pipes lie in the weeds are patient follow the exquisite
melodies there are seven hanging in the net now says the youngest
and cuts himself some ham

But when the full moon is behind clouds my brothers walk in the
woods with the dogs hold the branches back for each other see a
cracked enamel pot in the sky they lay their hands on the hickory tree
pluck a blade of grass blow deer out into the open and hit them as
they learned to with the first shot come groaning through the yard
with a load as stiff as a board on their backs

My brothers have got yellow greatcoats stars soft creased boots they
carry knapsacks there is a picture of our house packed inside a tin of
meat and their bird net they have the latest guns go abroad they are to
shoot when there is a man in the sights I know my brothers they hold
the branches back for each other and are patient right to the end

Dogtooth Violet Marsh Trefoil
Tr. *Agnes Stein*

Weeds the simple flowers
Have been uprooted
For some time to manicure the graves
The fallen iron crosses
The smooth hard stones
Give the dead a name, the number
Of their mortal lives I see
Much injustice, for example Marie
was only a fleeting guest
I count and it amounts to nothing

Devilish nonsense delusion miserable comfort oh Marie
Whether you aged in honor or misery
For years you have not walked the earth
Nettles rue and cinquefoil
Grow from the graves
The shells of snails in the grass lie empty.

Noon
Tr. Agnes Stein

Wild roses and blackberries
Send out their tender runners
Fever sweeps the garden, the poppy
Drugs itself and opens its capsule.
Blue bushes drop like lightning
Strokes over fences and the corpses
Of yellow banded wasps, numb
Crickets in the burning flowers
With their frightening eyes.

Pigs root black out
Of the green earth, they're reeling
An overflow of rotting pears
Has made them drunk they break out
Of the sty and scratch their backs
On the bark of scrub oaks.
The magpie breaks into a laugh lands
On my shoulder begs
An earring from me where the woods begin.

HELGA M. NOVAK

Tr. Agnes Stein

Punishment – Another Look

my bowed-down head
worries about the giraffe women
in the 'fabulous land'

they walk about
through grassy valleys
giraffe heads carried high
a hundred and more copper bands
one topping the other circle their necks

through the Kayah valleys
in-between three hills
their long necks sway
gleaming like old oil
but the swaying of their proud tops
is like rotten rye in the wind
never was the expression –
head high – so pointless
or – things will work out –

because only infidelity frees
the giraffe woman from bondage
the punishment for adultery is
the breaking apart of the copper bands
a neck without muscles and veins –
truly the race engenders
satanic blossoms
impossible ever to raise the head
impossible to scream
impossible to eat
the giraffe woman lies somewhere about
in one of the Kayah valleys
where infidelity is punished with hunger
she whose neck falls abruptly
to the side at the band's felling
can count her blessings
dead on the spot
and forgotten the valleys of Kayah

What a Wind

what a wind
that graphs the face

and tears the lips
what a wind
that strings an army out
hurling clubs between the legs
it rips the skin
off fields and earth
disrobes the oats
down to the original grain
potatoes are off on their travels
their eyes split
what a wind
that lifts the woodland oaks
dispersing shrubbery
what a wind
that in the spring of the year
sweeps the graveyard with a green broom

BETTINA WEGNER

Tr. Agnes Stein

The Enemy

The moon had a courtyard
into which they shoved cannons.
The sun had a light
of which they made torches.
The field was filled with corn
of which they made scrap.

The night had a coat
from which they cut camouflage.
The man had a fist
of which they made bombs.
The woman had a lap
which they named a tavern.

The children had clear vision
they knew their enemy
and made use of everything.

ÉILEAN NÍ CHUILLEANÁIN

Acts and Monuments

In imitation of the weed
Which, out of soft enclosing mud
As from a hand that holds a lead
Leans after the escaping flood,

Or when warm summer stunts the flow
In tangled coils lies tired and fine,
Or in calm weather stands tiptoe
To peer above the waterline,

The rooted trees bend in the wind
Or twist and bow on every side;
The poplar stands up straight and slim;
But their blood cannot flower or fade

Like weeds that rot when rivers dry.
Their roots embrace the stony plain,
Their branches move as one, they try
To freeze the effects of wind and rain.

And like the waterline the sky
Lids and defines the element
Where no unformed capricious cry
Can sound without its monument.

Wash

Wash man out of the earth; shear off
The human shell.
Twenty feet down there's close cold earth
So clean.

Wash the man out of the woman:
The strange sweat from her skin, the ashes from her hair.
Stretch her to dry in the sun
The blue marks on her breast will fade.

Woman and world not yet
Clean as the cat
Leaping to the windowsill with a fish in her teeth;
Her flat curious eyes reflect the squalid room,
She begins to wash the water from the fish.

More Islands

A child afraid of islands, their dry
Moonlit shoulders, sees in a deep gutter
A stone, a knot in the stream.
She feels the gasping of wrecks,
Cormorants and lighthouses.

She grows up to detest airports
But feels the sea in the waves of her hair
And icebergs in a storm of lemonade.

She knows there are some islands the sea avoids.
Boats leaving the coastline are led far astray
By strong currents, long mackerel shoals.
High on their dark rocks a man
Shouting for help, a bell ringing
Can call over hundreds of high tides
And not be heard, raising no echo
Until an injured seagull blown flat along the stones
Touches the hard earth, or the first fire
Lit by a castaway cuts the darkness
Liberating silence.

MEDBH MCGUCKIAN

Confinement

Child in the centre of the dark parquet,
Sleepy, glassed-in child, my fair copy,
While you were sailing your boat in the bay,
I saw you pass along the terrace twice,
Flying in the same direction as the epidemic
Of leaves in the hall. Our half-unpeopled
Household, convalescent from the summer's leap,
That indiscreetly drew the damp from walls,
And coaxed our neighbour, the forest, into this
Sorority, how could I share with you, unpruned
And woebegone? A swan bearing your shape
Re-entered the river imagery of my arms.

To the Nightingale

I remember our first night in this grey
And paunchy house: you were still slightly
In love with me, and dreamt of having
A grown son, your body in the semi-gloom
Turning my dead layers into something
Resembling a rhyme. That smart and
Cheerful rain almost beat the hearing
Out of me, and yet I heard my name
Pronounced in a whisper as a June day
Will force itself into every room.

To the nightingale it made no difference
Of course, that you tossed about an hour,
Two hours, till what was left of your future
Began; nor to the moon that nearly rotted,
Like the twenty-first century growing
Its grass through me. But became in the end,
While you were still asleep, a morning
Where I saw our neighbours' mirabelle,

Bent over our hedge, and its trespassing
Fruit, unacknowledged as our own.

Vanessa's Bower

I will tell you words which you will
Probably soon afterwards throw out of
Your head, where everything is in order,
And in bloom, like the bird-cherry reading
In a frostless climate, or the cheerfulness
Of ships being wooed by the sea away from
My possessive arm. Dear owner, you write,
Don't put me into your pocket, I am not
A willow in your folly-studded garden,
Which you hope will weep the right way:
And there are three trains leaving, none
Of which connects me to your E-shaped
Cottage. Alas, I have still the feeling,
Half-fatherly, half-different, we are
Travelling together in the train with this letter
Though my strange hand will never be your sin.

From the Dressing-Room

Left to itself, they say, every foetus
Would turn female, staving in, nature
Siding then with the enemy that
Delicately mixes up genders. This
Is an absence I have passionately sought,
Brightening nevertheless my poet's attic
With my steady hands, calling him my blue
Lizard till his moans might be heard
At the far end of the garden. For I like
His ways, he's light on his feet and does
Not break anything, puts his entire soul
Into bringing me a glass of water.

I can take anything now, even his being
Away, for it always seems to me his

Writing is for me, as I walk springless
From the dressing-room in a sisterly
Length of flesh-coloured silk. Oh there
Are moments when you think you can
Give notice in a jolly, wifely tone,
Tossing off a very last and sunsetty
Letter of farewell, with strict injunctions
To be careful to procure his own lodgings,
That my good little room is lockable,
But shivery, I recover at the mere
Sight of him propping up my pillow.

EAVAN BOLAND

Naoise at Four

The trap baited for them snaps.
Like forest pests they fall for it,
Like humans writhe, like both submit.
Three brothers die, their three saps
Spill until their split kith
Heals into an Irish myth.

Naoise, named for one of these,
You stand in our kitchen, sip
Milk from a mottled cup
From our cupboard. Our unease
Vanishes with one smile
As each suburban, modern detail

Distances us from old lives
Old deaths, but nightly on our screen
New ones are lost, wounds open,
And I despair of what perspective
On this sudden Irish fury
Will solve it to a folk memory.

Godson, little creditor,
Your spiritual good in trust

To me demands at very least
I be your spirit's auditor
Until the moment you first try
To make your own inventory.

Your father gossips of the wood
Around your house, a lucky context
Where values can be learned, fixed,
A truce with life negotiated
On terms you yourself can make
Unlike your luckless namesake.

You drain your cup; your love
Is a closed circuit like your glove
In your mother's. There is nothing to sell you
Here, invest in nothing: at home
Badgers, voles enrich your time:
Your currency will not devalue.

On Renoir's 'The Grape-Pickers'

They seem to be what they are harvesting:
Rumps, elbows, hips clustering
Plumply in the sun, a fuss of shines
Wining from the ovals of their elbows.
The brush plucks them from a tied vine.
Such roundness, such a sound vintage
Of circles, such a work of pure spheres!
Flesh and shadow mesh inside each other.

But not this one: This red-headed woman.
Her skirt's a wave gathered to the weather
Of her brief sleep; her eyes are closed;
Her ears fisted in a dozed listening –
A dream of stoves and raked leaves and plums.
When she wakes summer will be over.

After a Childhood away from Ireland

One summer
we slipped in at dawn
on plum-coloured water
in the sloppy quiet.

The engines
of the ship stopped.
There was an eerie
drawing near,

a noiseless coming head-on
of red roofs, walls,
dogs, barley stooks.
Then we were there.

Cobh.
Coming home.
I had heard of this:
the ground the emigrants

resistless, weeping
laid their cheeks to,
put their lips to kiss.
Love is also memory.

I only stared.
What I had lost
was not land
but the habit

of land,
whether of growing out of,
or settling back on,
or being defined by.

I climb
to your nursery.
I stand listening
to the dissonances

of the summer's day ending.
I bend to kiss you.
Your cheeks are brick pink.
They store warmth like clay.

VLADIMÍRA ČEREPKOVÁ

Tr. George Theiner

Man and his Truth

You never knew a meadow
diluted by the sun
you never knew a pool
with stars in its depths
you never knew a stone
embedded in the ditch

First of all you wanted to know
the truth
you sought it in books
questioned your elders
argued with the young

Above your head only ceilings
but no sky
under your feet just floors
but no earth

You wanted to know the truth
you found it
just as you wanted it
standing on three spindly legs

And when that evening the sun went down
your truth was buried by its weight

GERDA MAYER

Monkey on the Analyst's Couch
(with a nod to Martin Bell's more handsome ape)

They photograph me
they show me to their students

And here's a monkey
deprived of love
he has nowhere to flee to
except his own arms

Now

I'm not naive
when the other monkeys approach
I know I should bristle or better
be friendly but firm or nonchalantly
pick a peanut from the floor
thoughtfully chew it
when they bare their teeth bare mine
ferocious or pleasant as the occasion calls for

Instead I panic
my hands fly to my head
I crouch   I cringe   it is
too tempting a stance for them
yes, even for the nicest of monkeys

A submissive rump
asking to be kicked
they kick   I submit
I submit   they kick

15th March 1939

And she said
The Germans have marched into Prague
And she said
THE GER-MANS HAVE MARCHED IN-TO PRAGUE

Careless, eleven,
I smile comprehension.
(Or was it embarrassment?
Or was it a not-wanting-to-know?
How can I tell now
so many years later?)
And I wrote in my letter
What are
the German uniforms like?
And my father replying,
(and my father forgiving me):
Not bad
as uniforms go.

Poem About Something

When we were newly married, coy and young,
We did not fornicate, copulate, or even
'Make Love'. No – we *had*
Something; saying 'we had something
Last night', in the bickering dawn, to
Recapitulate love. Then (as not now) we
'Had something' on the new lino, in each new
Bed, you, afterwards, hopping, to spatter
In blessing the last seeds. In the
Conjugal bath we had something that
Churned the deeps and drowned the bathroom
Floor, and on Scottish hills, spotted
With grey wool tufts what we had
Only the sheep could tell. Now
What we have is confined to bed
And propriety. The lino's replaced,
The new kitchen floor unsanctified. You
No longer kiss me from my feet upwards and no
Wonder, seeing my bunion, my wrestler's thigh . . .
                                                            But

Broadminded now, what we do is to fuck
Conscientiously and to keep in

Practice. We've had something,
I think.

DESANKA MAKSIMOVIĆ

Tr. Vasa D. Mihailovich

For Lies Spoken out of Kindness

I seek mercy
for those who lack the courage
to tell the evil one that he is evil
or the bad one that he is bad,
for those who hesitate
to hurt with the truth,
for the people who lie out of kindness.
For the man who would rather be humiliated
than humiliate,
for the man who has no heart
to pull down a mask when he sees it
on someone's face,
for people who cannot insult
those of different thoughts and creeds,
for those who never could
pronounce a sentence to others,
for whom all judges seem strict,
for every kind untruthful story
and other similar weaknesses.

Now it is Certain

Through the same gate I shall enter too.
The shadow will rush toward me
as one always rushes to a newcomer
arriving from the region
from which we were banished.

Their faces will be both different
and the same,

as every night the face of the moon
is different and the same again.

But I shall recognize your faces
were they woven of darkness
or shining with an inner glow;
they'll give themselves away by a small sign,
perhaps by a smile they had on the earth,
perhaps by the familiar sorrow in the eyes,
perhaps by the arch of the eyebrow.

VESNA PARUN

Tr. Vasa D. Mihailovich and Moran

A House on the Road

I lay in the dust by the road
neither did I see his face
nor did he see mine.

The stars descended and the air was blue.
Neither did I see his hands
nor did he see mine.

The east turned green like a lemon.
Because of a bird I opened my eyes.
Then I recognized whom I have loved
all my life.
Then he realized whose poor hands
he has hugged.

And the man took his bundle and set out
crying for his home.
And his home is the dust on the road,
just as mine.

GRACE NICHOLS

Wind a Change

Wind a change
blow soft but
steadfast

ripple the spears
of sugar cane
stir slow the leaves
of indigo

Dance
waltz
soothe
this old mud-wattle
hut
bring if you can
the smell of Dahomey
again

Wind a change
cool mountain water
open river flower

But pass easy
up the big house
way
let them sleep
they happy white sleep

Yes, Wind a change
keep yuh coming fire
secret

The Return

Is that you Nanny
Is that you Black Priestess

Is that your Abeng voice
echoing its warcry through the valleys?

Like Anansi

I was the Ashanti spider

woman-keeper
of dreams
tenacious
opalescent
dark eyes
unblinking

waiting
with a long
and naked fury

then you came
like Anansi
you came

calm and cunning
as a madman

not at all
what I was expecting

bells hung
from your little waist
an ornate flute

beads and feathers
stood in your cap
and I laughed at you

Old Magic

She, the mirror
you break in seven pieces

the curse you think
you leave behind

the woman make young
with old magic

the one you going
sleep with

the one you going
think is kind

Waterpot

The daily going out
and coming in
always being hurried
along
like like . . . cattle

In the evenings
returning from the fields
she tried hard to walk
like a woman

she tried very hard
pulling herself erect
with every three or four
steps
pulling herself together
holding herself like
royal cane

And the overseer
hurrying them along
in the quickening darkness

And the overseer sneering
them along in the quickening
darkness

sneered at the pathetic –
the pathetic display
of dignity

O but look
there's a waterpot growing
from her head

RUTH MILLER

Fruit

These were the distant fruits of a garden childhood:
Yellow fluff on the hard astringent quince –
Finger-scratched to smooth small streets and lanes;
Cornelian-coloured ball of pomegranate,
Split in shining cups of pirate rubies
Set each against each like bee-cells in white silk;
Figs that we shredded, pulpy soft and purple,
Throwing aside the dry and skeined imposters,
Their milkflesh stained with russet short-cut threads.

Sunday fruit was silver-bought. But these
Grew in the garden, formed a roadside hedge,
Concealed us from the coinage of the world.
Amongst the quince, the fig, the pomegranate
We hid away with glossy greensprung secrets;
Lay quiet and heavy, sweet with an edge of bitter
Under the lazy heat, the languorous season:
Breathless to be plucked and by love consumed.

Penguin on the Beach

Stranger in his own element,
Sea-casualty, the castaway manikin
Waddles in his tailored coat-tails. Oil

Has spread a deep commercial stain
Over his downy shirtfront. Sleazy, grey,
It clogs the sleekness. Far too well

He must recall the past, to be so cautious:
Watch him step into the waves. He shudders
Under the froth, slides, slips, on the wet sand,

Escaping to dryness, dearth, in a white cascade,
An involuntary shouldering off of gleam.
Hands push him back into the sea. He stands

In pained and silent expostulation.
Once he knew a sunlit, leaping smoothness,
But close within his head's small knoll, and dark

He retains the image: oil on sea,
Green slicks, black lassos of sludge
Sleaving the breakers in a stain-spread scarf.

He shudders now from the clean flinching wave,
Turns and plods back up the yellow sand,
Ineffably weary, triumphantly sad.

He is immensely wise: he trusts nobody. His senses
Are clogged with experience. He eats
Fish from his Saviour's hands, and it tastes black.

CONTRIBUTORS' NOTES

U. A. FANTHORPE Born 1929 in Kent. Now lives in Gloucestershire. Publications: *Side Effects*; *Standing To* (Peterloo Poets, 1978, 1982).

ANNE STEVENSON Born 1933 in Cambridge. Brought up in the USA, now lives in England. Publications: *Living in America* (1965); *Reversals* (1969), both published in USA. *Correspondences* (1974); *Travelling Behind Glass – Selected Poems 1963–73* (1974); *Enough of Green* (1977); *Minute by Glass Minute* (1982), all from Oxford University Press.

ELIZABETH BARTLETT Born 1924 in Kent. Now lives in Sussex. Publications: *A Lifetime of Dying*; *Strange Territory* (Peterloo Poets, 1979, 1983).

FLEUR ADCOCK Born 1934 in New Zealand, came to England 1963. Publications: *The Eye of the Hurricane* (1963); *Tigers* (1967); *High Tide in the Garden* (1971); *The Scenic Route* (1974); *The Inner Harbour* (1979); *Selected Poems* (1983), all from Oxford University Press. *Below Loughrigg*; *The Virgin and the Nightingale* (Bloodaxe, 1979, 1983).

VICKI FEAVER Born 1943 in Nottinghamshire. Read music at Durham University. Publication: *Close Relatives* (Secker & Warburg, 1981).

PATRICIA BEER Born 1924 in Devon. Now lives in London. Publications: *Loss of the Magyar and Other Poems*; *The Survivors* (Longman, 1959, 1963). *Just Like the Resurrection*; *The Estuary* (Macmillan, 1967, 1971). *Driving West* (Gollancz, 1975). *Poems, 1967–79* (Hutchinson, 1979).

JEAN EARLE Born 1909 in Bristol, brought up in Rhondda Valley, now lives in Dyfed. Publication: *A Trial of Strength* (Carcanet, 1980).

WENDY COPE Born 1945 in Kent. Now lives in London. A selection of her poems is included in *Poetry Introduction 5* (Faber, 1981), *The Sweet and Sour Anthology* (Batsford, 1983) and *New Poetry 9* (The Arts Council, 1983).

ELMA MITCHELL Born 1919 in Airdrie, Scotland, now lives in Somerset. Publications: *The Poor Man in the Flesh*; *The Human Cage* (Peterloo Poets, 1976, 1979).

SELIMA HILL Born 1945 in London, where she still lives. Publication: *Saying Hello at the Station* (Chatto & Windus, 1984).

ALISON BRACKENBURY Born 1953 in Lincolnshire. Publications: *Dreams of Power* (1981); *Breaking Ground* (1984); also featured in *Some Contemporary Poets of Britain and Ireland* (1984), all from Carcanet.

GWEN HARWOOD Born 1920 in Brisbane, Queensland, Australia. Publications: *Poems* (1963); *Poems Vol. Two* (1968); *New and Selected Poems* (1974); *The Lion's Bride* (1981), all from Angus and Robertson.

ANTIGONE KEFALA Born 1939 in Romania, of Greek parents. Attended schools in Greece, moved to New Zealand where she attended University, settled in Australia in 1969. Publications: volumes from small presses, translations and two novels.

JILL HELLYER Born 1925 in Sydney, Australia. Publications: *The Exile* (Alpha Press, 1969); *Song of the Humpback Whales* (Sisters Publishing Ltd., 1981), and one novel.

DOROTHY HEWETT Born 1923 in Perth, Australia. Publications: many volumes of poetry, plays, one novel and one volume of collected short stories. Poetry includes *Rapunzel in Suburbia* (Prism, 1975).

ANNA SWIRSZCZYNSKA Born 1909 in Warsaw but had lived in Cracow since the war. Died in 1984. Publications: *I am Baba* (1972) and *Building a Barricade* (1974).

ASTRIDE IVASKA Born 1926 in Latvia. Publications: *Judgement of Winter* (1968); *A Step into the Forest* (1973). The translations here are from *At the Fallows Edge* (Santa Barbara Press, 1981); also in *East European Poetry* (Ardis, 1984).

ANA BLANDIANA Born 1942 in Romania. Publications: *First Person Plural* (1964); *Fifty Poems* (1970) and *The Sleep in Sleep* (1977).

GABRIELA MELINESCU Born 1942 in Bucharest but now lives in Sweden.

NATALYA GORBANEVSKAYA Born 1936 in Russia. Has written much but only nine of her poems have been published in 'official' Soviet Journals. She was imprisoned in a psychiatric hospital after demonstrating in Red Square against the invasion of Czechoslovakia in 1968. Her *Selected Poems* are published by Carcanet, 1972.

BELLA AKHMADULINA Born 1937 in Moscow. Publications: *String* (1962) which was criticised by the Government; *The Rain* (1963); *My Ancestry* (1964); *Summer Leaves* (1968); *Music Lessons* (1969); *Fever* (Owen, 1970). She was married to Yevtushenko and is now divorced.

YUNNA MORITZ Born 1937 in Kiev. Her first collection appeared when she was 20, and she has published many since.

NOVELLA MATVEYEVA Born 1935 in Russia. She was brought up in a children's home and spent much of her time in hospitals. Publications: *The Soul of Things* (in Russian, 1966) and several other volumes.

MARIANNE MOORE Born 1887 in St. Louis, Missouri. Died 1972. Her first book of poems was published in 1927. She has won many awards, including the Pulitzer Prize for poetry in 1951. Her *Collected Poems* published by Faber & Faber (1968).

ELIZABETH BISHOP Born 1911 in Nova Scotia. Died 1979. Publications include: *Complete Poems 1927–1979*; *Collected Prose* (Chatto & Windus, 1983, 1984).

ADRIENNE RICH Born 1929 in Baltimore. Publications: many volumes of poetry, including *Selected Poems* (Chatto & Windus, 1967) and also celebrated pioneer feminist works.

MARILYN HACKER Born 1942 in New York City. Publications: several volumes of poetry, including *Presentation Piece*; *Separations* (Alfred Knopf, 1974, 1976).

BARBARA GUEST Born 1920, lives in New York City. Publications: *The Locations of Things* (1960) and six further volumes. The poems included here are from *Moscow Mansions* (Viking, 1973).

LOUISE GLÜCK Born 1943, New York City. Publications include: *Firstborn*; *The House on the Marshland* (Ecco Press, New York City, 1967, 1975). Both books are reprinted in England by Anvil Press Poetry.

CELIA GILBERT Born 1932 in America. Publications: *Queen of Darkness* (Viking, 1977). *Bonfire* (Alice James Books, 1983). The poems here are from *Bonfire*.

BEATRICE HAWLEY Born 1944 in America. Publications: *Nothing is Lost* (Apple-Wood Press, 1979), and *Making the House Fall Down* (Alice James Books, 1983).

AMY CLAMPITT Born in New Providence, Iowa, lives in New York. Publications: *The Kingfisher* (Alfred Knopf, USA, 1983). Reprinted in England by Faber & Faber.

CAROLYN FORCHÉ Born in El Salvador, lives in America. Publications: *Gathering the Tribes* (1976), which won a Yale award. Also *The Country Between Us* (Harper & Row, New York, 1982; Cape, London, 1983).

CLARIBEL ALEGRÍA Born in Nicaragua but has lived most of her life in El Salvador. She has published many volumes of poetry and was awarded the 'Casa de las Americas' prize for *Sobrevivo* (1978).

KATHLEEN JAMIE Born 1962 in Renfrew, Scotland. Publications: *Black Spiders* (Salamander Press, 1982).

VALERIE GILLIES Born in Canada, brought up in Scotland. Publications: *Each Bright Eye*; *Bed of Stone* (Canongate Press, Edinburgh, 1977, 1984).

LIZ LOCHHEAD Born 1947 in Scotland. Publications: *Memo for Spring* (Reprographia, 1972). The poems here are from *The Grim Sisters* (Next Editions).

ÁGNES GERGELY Born 1933 in Hungary. Publications: She has published five volumes of poetry, some novels and many works in translation (English–Hungarian).

MARGARET ATWOOD Born 1939 in Ottawa. Publications: eleven volumes of poetry, seven of fiction, criticism and children's books. The poems included here are all from *The Animals in that Country* (OUP, Toronto, 1968).

MIRIAM WADDINGTON Born 1917 in Canada. Publications: *Green World* (1945) and many more since.

JENNY MASTORÁKI Born 1949 in Athens. Publications: *The Long-Winded Story of Holy Youth* (1972); *The Lineage* (1978).

DAHLIA RAVIKOVITCH Born 1936 in Israel. Publications: *The Love of an Orange* (1959) and four other volumes of poetry; also translations and children's books.

RIVKA MIRIAM Born 1952 in Israel. Publications: *My Yellow Robe* (1966) and three other volumes.

EUNICE DE SOUZA Born in India. Publications: include *Fix* (Newground, 1979), from which the poem was taken.

SARAH KIRSCH Born 1935 in Limlingerode, East Germany. Studied and worked in East Germany until 1977, now lives in West Berlin. Publications: ten books of poetry, many translations, e.g. Tsvetaeva and Akhmatova.

HELGA M. NOVAK Born 1935 in East Germany. Poems here are from *Margarete mit dem Schrank* (1978), translated by Agnes Stein.

BETTINA WEGNER Born 1947 in East Germany. The poem here is from *Wenn Meine Lieder Nicht Mehr Stimmen* (1980) translated by Agnes Stein.

ÉILEAN NÍ CHUILLEANÁIN Born 1942 in Cork. Now a lecturer at Trinity College, Dublin. The poems here are from *Acts and Monuments* (Gallery Press, Dublin, 1972), and *The Second Voyage* (Wake Forest University Press, 1977).

MEDBH MCGUCKIAN Born 1950 in Belfast. Publications: *The Shadow Master*; *Venus and the Rain* (OUP, Oxford, 1982, 1984).

EAVAN BOLAND Born 1944 in Ireland. Publications: *New Territory*; *The War Horse* (Gollancz, 1967, 1975). The poems here are from *Night Feed* (Arlen House, Dublin, 1982), and *The War Horse*.

VLADIMÍRA ČEREPKOVÁ Born 1946 in Czechoslovakia. The poem here is from *Fish Speaks to Fish* (1969), translated by George Theiner.

GERDA MAYER Born 1927 in Czechoslovakia, moved to London when young and attended Bedford College, University of London. Publications include: *Monkey on the Analyst's Couch* (Ceolfrith Press, 1980).

DESANKA MAKSIMOVIĆ Born 1898 in Yugoslavia, studied in Belgrade and Paris. Began to publish her work after World War II. Many works in print including *Poet in his Native Land* (1946), and *I have no more time* (1973).

VESNA PARUN Born 1922 in Yugoslavia. Publications include: *I was a boy* (1962), *The Wind of Thrace* (1964) and *Accursed Rain* (1969).

GRACE NICHOLS Born 1950 in Guyana. Has lived in England since 1977. Her first collection was *I is a Long Memoried Woman* (Caribbean Cultural International, London, 1983), from which these poems were taken. Her poems also appear in *News for Babylon: The Chatto Book of Westindian-British Poetry*, edited by James Berry (Chatto & Windus, 1984).

RUTH MILLER Born 1919 in Cape Province, South Africa, died 1969. Publications: *Floating Island* (Humon & Rousseau, 1965); *Selected Poems* (Chatto & Windus, 1968).

ACKNOWLEDGEMENTS

The editor and publishers gratefully acknowledge permission to reprint copyright material as follows:

U. A. FANTHORPE Poems are from *Standing To* (Peterloo Poets, 1982).

ANNE STEVENSON 'By the Boat House, Oxford', 'Thales and Li Po', and 'A Summer Place' are from *Enough of Green* (Oxford University Press, 1977), 'Suicide' is from *Minute by Glass Minute* (Oxford University Press, 1982).

ELIZABETH BARTLETT Poems are from *A Lifetime of Dying* (Peterloo Poets, 1979).

FLEUR ADCOCK Poems are from *Selected Poems* (Oxford University Press, 1983).

VICKI FEAVER 'Mr Sparke' is from *Close Relatives* (Secker & Warburg, 1981).

PATRICIA BEER Poems are from *Poems, 1967–79* (Hutchinson, 1979).

JEAN EARLE Poems are from *A Trial of Strength* (Carcanet Press, 1980).

WENDY COPE The 'Strugnell Sonnets' are from *The Sweet and Sour Anthology* (Batsford, 1983), and *New Poetry 9* (The Arts Council, 1983).

ELMA MITCHELL 'Late Fall' and 'Thoughts after Ruskin' are from *The Poor Man in the Flesh* (Peterloo Poets, 1976). 'Instead of a Flag' is from *The Human Cage* (Peterloo Poets, 1979).

SELIMA HILL Poems are from *Saying Hello at the Station* (Chatto & Windus, 1984).

ALISON BRACKENBURY 'Medine in Turkey' is from *Some Contemporary Poets of Britain and Ireland* (Carcanet, 1984); and 'Two Gardeners' is from *Dreams of Power* (Carcanet, 1981).

GWEN HARWOOD Poems are from the anthology, *Journeys* (Sisters Publishing Ltd., Carlton South, Victoria, Australia, 1982).

ANTIGONE KEFALA Poems are from *Mrs Noah and the Minoan Queen* (Sisters Publishing Ltd., 1983).

JILL HELLYER Poems are from *Song of the Humpback Whales* (Sisters Publishing Ltd., 1981).

DOROTHY HEWETT Poems are from the anthology, *Journeys* (Sisters Publishing Ltd., 1982).

ANNA SWIRSZCZYNSKA Poems are from *I am Baba*, translated by Margaret Marshment and Grazyra Baran (published by Wydawnictwo Literaekie).

ASTRIDE IVASKA Poems are from *East European Poetry*, trans. Inara Cedrins (Ardis, Ann Arbor, Michigan, USA, 1984).

ANA BLANDIANA Poems are from *East European Poetry*, trans. Michael Impey (Ardis, 1984).

GABRIELA MELINESCU Poems are from *A Book of Women Poets from Antiquity to Now*, trans. W. B. and Matei Calinescu (Schocken Books, New York, 1980).

NATALYA GORBANEVSKAYA Poems are from *Selected Poems*, trans. Daniel Weissbort (Carcanet, 1972).

BELLA AKHMADULINA 'The Bride', trans. Stephen Stepanchev, and 'Small Aircraft', trans. Daniel Halpern are from *A Book of Women Poets from Antiquity to Now* (Schocken, 1980). 'Fever', trans. Elaine Feinstein, is from *Three Russian Poets* (Carcanet, 1979).

YUNNA MORITZ Poems are from *Three Russian Poets*, trans. Elaine Feinstein (Carcanet, 1979).

NOVELLA MATVEYEVA Poems are from *Russian Poetry, the Modern Period*, trans. Daniel Weissbort (University of Iowa Press, 1978).

MARIANNE MOORE Poems are from *The Complete Poems* (Faber & Faber, 1968 and Macmillan Publishing Co. Inc., New York).

ELIZABETH BISHOP Poems are from *Complete Poems 1927–1979* (Chatto & Windus, and Farrar, Straus & Giroux, Inc., New York 1983).

ADRIENNE RICH Poems are from *Selected Poems* (Chatto & Windus, 1967 and W. W. Norton and Company, Inc., New York).

MARILYN HACKER Poems are from *Separations* (Alfred Knopf Inc., New York, 1976).

BARBARA GUEST Poems are from *Moscow Mansions* (Viking, 1973).

LOUISE GLÜCK Poems are from *The House on the Marshland* (Ecco Press, New York, and Anvil Press Poetry, 1975).

CELIA GILBERT Poems are from *Bonfire* (Alice James Books, Cambridge, Massachusetts, 1983).

BEATRICE HAWLEY Poems are from *Making the House Fall Down* (Alice James Books, 1983).

AMY CLAMPITT Poems are from *The Kingfisher* (Alfred Knopf, 1983; Faber & Faber, 1984).

CAROLYN FORCHÉ Poems are from *The Country Between Us* (Harper & Row Publishers Inc., New York, 1982; Jonathan Cape, 1983).

CLARIBEL ALEGRÍA Poems are from *Index on Censorship*, 2/84.

KATHLEEN JAMIE Poems are from *Black Spiders* (Salamander Press, 1982).

VALERIE GILLIES Poems are from *Bed of Stone* (Canongate, 1984).

LIZ LOCHHEAD Poems are from *The Grimm Sisters* (Next Editions, 1981).

ÁGNES GERGELY Poems are from *Modern Hungarian Poetry* (Columbia University Press, 1977); 'Crazed Man In Concentration Camp', trans. Edwin Morgan, and 'Sign on My Door Jamb', trans. Thomas Land.

MARGARET ATWOOD Poems are from *The Animals in That Country* (Oxford University Press, Toronto, 1968).

MIRIAM WADDINGTON Poems are from *The Price of Gold* (Oxford University Press, Toronto, 1976).

JENNY MASTORÁKI Poems are from *A Book of Women Poets from Antiquity to Now* (Schocken Books, 1980). 'The Vandals', and 'Prometheus', trans. Nikos Germanakos; 'The Death of a Warrior', trans. Kimon Friar.

DAHLIA RAVIKOVITCH Poems are from *The Literary Review*, Vol. 26, 1983, trans. Chana Bloch (Fairleigh Dickinson University Press, Madison, New Jersey, USA).

RIVKA MIRIAM Poems are from *The Literary Review*, Vol. 26, 1983, trans. Linda Zisquit (Fairleigh Dickinson University).

EUNICE DE SOUZA Poems are from *Fix* (Newground, India, 1979).
SARAH KIRSCH 'Before the Sun Rises' is from *An Anthology of East German Poetry*; 'Dogtooth Violet Marsh Trefoil' and 'Noon' are from *Erdreich* (1982) trans. Agnes Stein.
HELGA M. NOVAK Poems are from *Margarete mit dem Schrank*, trans. Agnes Stein (Rotbuch Verlag, Berlin, West Germany, 1978).
BETTINA WEGNER The poem is from *Wenn Meine Lieder Nicht Mehr Stimmen*, trans. Agnes Stein (Rowohlt Verlag, Reinbek, Hamburg, West Germany, 1980).
ÉILEAN NÍ CHUILLEANÁIN Poems are from *Acts and Monuments* (Gallery Press, Dublin, 1972), and *The Second Voyage* (Wake Forest University Press, Winston-Salem, North Carolina, USA, 1977).
MEDBH MCGUCKIAN Poems are from *Venus and the Rain* (Oxford University Press, 1984).
EAVAN BOLAND 'Naoise at Four' is from *The War Horse* (Gollancz, 1975); 'On Renoir's "The Grape-Pickers"', and 'After a Childhood Away from Ireland' are from *Night Feed* (Arlen House, Dublin, 1982).
VLADIMÍRA ČEREPKOVÁ The poem is from *Fish Speaks to Fish*, trans. George Theiner (1969).
GERDA MAYER Poems are from *Monkey on the Analyst's Couch* (Ceolfrith, 1980).
DESANKA MAKSIMOVIĆ Poems are from *Contemporary Yugoslav Poetry*, trans. D. Mihailovich (University of Iowa Press, 1977).
VESNA PARUN The poem is from *Contemporary Yugoslav Poetry*, trans. D. Mihailovich and Moran (University of Iowa Press, 1977).
GRACE NICHOLS Poems are from *I is a Long Memoried Woman* (Caribbean Cultural International, 1983).
RUTH MILLER Poems are from *Selected Poems* (Chatto & Windus, 1968).